Memories
Before and After
The Sound of Music

AN AUTOBIOGRAPHY

Agathe von Trapp

With Illustrations by the Author

WITHDRAWN

HARPER

NEW YORK · LONDON · TORONTO · SYDNEY

HARPER

This book was first published in 2004 by PublishAmerica, LLLP.

Scripture verses are from the Holy Bible, King James Version.

HarperCollins books may be purchased for educational, business, or sales promotional use. For information please write: Special Markets Department, HarperCollins Publishers, 10 East 53rd Street, New York, NY 10022.

FIRST HARPER PAPERBACK PUBLISHED 2010.

Library of Congress Cataloging-in-Publication Data is available upon request.

ISBN 978-0-06-199881-2

10 11 12 13 14   QCF   10 9 8 7 6 5 4 3 2 1

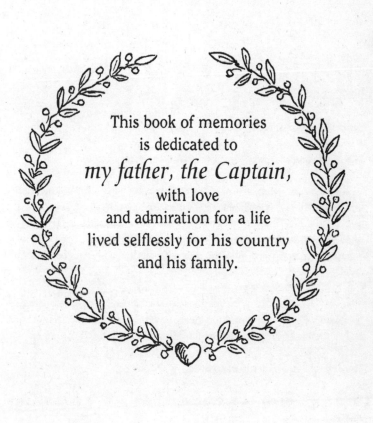

This book of memories
is dedicated to
my father, the Captain,
with love
and admiration for a life
lived selflessly for his country
and his family.

Contents

Acknowledgments

*I*t is one of my life experiences that when someone starts a project and others think it is worthwhile, help comes from all sides until the project has reached completion. I believe that this is what happened with my memories when I began to write them down. I would like to extend my gratitude to all the kind and knowledgeable people whose efforts helped to bring my memories into print. Therefore, I wish to say to everyone who assisted me along the way, "I sincerely thank you!"

Special thanks and gratitude to my friends Janet and Alan Yuspeh, without whose interest, help, and encouragement this book would not have been possible. I appreciate Alan's patience, our phone consultations, and all the meals we shared. I will always remember Janet fondly when I think of our many valuable and enjoyable work sessions.

Heartfelt thanks to my faithful friend, Mary Lou Kane, who worked tirelessly in countless ways. Her energy and support enabled me to complete this ambitious project. In our long sessions, Mary Lou and Janet helped me to clarify and translate my images and memories into the book's current form. Of course, "tea with jam and bread," contributed by Janet, sweetened the process.

I am especially grateful to my brothers and sisters for their wholehearted support of my efforts to record my memories of the life we shared for so many years and for their assistance with Chapter 18. My sister Maria, my sister-in-law Erika, and my brother Johannes were always happy to help my fading memory. Also, Maria provided me with special photographs.

A sincere thank you to William T. Anderson for his many hours of work in preliminary editing, chapter restructuring, and providing suggestions, photos, concert reviews, and programs.

My appreciation to Hirsch Goldberg for his interest, suggestions, and preliminary editing.

My special thanks go to University Docent Dr. Walter Brunner for sending me "The Wedding" from the archives in Graz, Austria.

Thank you to Sara DiRienzi for typing the manuscript; Ryan Hulvat for the photo of The von Trapp Children in concert; and Anita and Steve Shevett for the photo of my eighty-fifth birthday.

My sincere thanks for their help and encouragement to Ruth Miriam Carey, S.S.N.D., Joyce DiRienzi, Catherine R. Engers, Kathleen Marie Engers, S.S.N.D., Suzanne Ford, Louis Hillman, Susan Kessler, Emmett Sinnott, and Jane Weaver.

Last, but not least, my gratitude and appreciation to my editorial consultant, D. B. Kellogg, who patiently guided me through the many steps along the way and worked day and night as we prepared the manuscript for publication.

Prelude

henever I meet people and it dawns on them that I am a member of the actual von Trapp Family whose story inspired *The Sound of Music*, I am confronted with questions: "Who are you in the movie?" "Are the play and the movie authentic?" "Did you escape from the Nazis over the mountains?" Then people want to know all about my family and our lives before and after the era depicted in *The Sound of Music* (the stage play and the film). This interest is always genuine, and is touching to me.

But how can I tell the story of our large family and its adventures that took place over a period of more than a hundred years in a few minutes of conversation? Our life story has been told, reported on, and adapted ever since we first arrived in America to give concerts in 1938. Many people know of us as the Trapp Family Singers from our concerts, our record albums, and the Broadway play and motion picture based on our life story. Others are familiar with us because of the books written by my second mother, Maria Augusta von Trapp. Thousands have attended our music camp or visited the still operating Trapp Family Lodge in Stowe, Vermont.

Our story has also been distorted at times, with not only *The Sound of Music* resorting to a liberal dose of artistic license, but also many articles being written with incorrect information about our family. And since my second mother joined our family after seven of us children had already been born, her books do not reflect what our earlier life was like, our father's and grandfather's impressive histories, or our first mother's important role. Nor do the books based on Maria's story depict what transpired after she passed away in

1987. Indeed, few people know much about our lives before and after *The Sound of Music* became one of the most popular musicals of all time.

As the oldest daughter of Georg Ritter von Trapp and his first wife, Agathe Whitehead von Trapp, I have long felt a need to answer the many questions posed to our family over the years and to respond to the widespread desire to learn more about our story that has fascinated so many.

I have often been asked to write down my memories of the untold era of our lives—the period of World War I and its aftermath—when we lived in the secure home of our maternal grandmother. Looking back, I am grateful that we were allowed to take our first steps into the world in one of Austria's most beautiful areas, the shore of a lake surrounded by high mountains.

In this book, I will tell of our early years, of the invasion of Austria and how it changed our lives, of our life in America, of our tours as the Trapp Family Singers, of my reactions to *The Sound of Music*, and I will give an update on each of my brothers and sisters. I want to point out that these are *my* memories; my siblings may remember certain events differently, which is only natural because individuals may experience the same event in different ways. And as the oldest daughter, I lived through more of the family's history than most of my brothers and sisters.

My family lived through some of the twentieth century's most trying times without compromising our deeply held beliefs. Often when the problems we faced seemed insurmountable and overwhelming, circumstances would suddenly change for the better to smooth our way into the next step of our journey. Some people would call these positively changed circumstances "coincidences." I, however, do not think of them as such. Throughout the turbulent years of war and other difficulties, God's guidance and protection kept us safe in the palm of His hand.

Agathe von Trapp
Baltimore, Maryland, 2002

1

The Captain, Our Father

The Austria of my childhood was Austria at war. During World War I, which began in 1914, our father, Georg von Trapp, was the commander of a submarine. He was not only an outstanding commander in the Austrian Navy, a man of vision, courage, and exceptional presence of mind, but also a loving husband and father.

Papá was tall with a slender, well-proportioned build. Distinguished in appearance, he had dark hair, a mustache, and brown eyes that commanded attention in a gentle manner. His hands were strong, well shaped, and accentuated by his engagement and wedding rings. Attentive and sensitive to his surroundings, Papá walked erect and moved easily.

He looked good in whatever he wore. Papá's clothes were always neat, clean, and well coordinated. As for colors, he wore mostly a mild, muted green. His suits were made of wool tweed. The trousers were knickers, according to the fashion of his time (between 1914 and 1925). Since the knickers reached only below the knees, men in those days wore knee-high stockings knitted in different patterns. These were overturned on the top to hide the garters. Jackets, vests, and trousers were of the same material and color. A white shirt with a tie completed the outfit. In the summer, Papá wore the traditional *Lederhosen* (short pants made of leather), a white shirt, and a gray jacket. The jacket was of a lighter woolen material, with moss green cuffs and a standing collar. Papá wore knitted knee-highs, even in the summer, and brown shoes. To me, he always looked handsome.

Papá was not only kind and loving to us, but also polite to strangers and a true friend to his friends and the crews of his ships. One could count on his word. Naturally dignified, he was not dependent upon what other people thought of him but lived his life according to his conscience. He always showed genuine friendliness. He did not have to say to us, "I love you." We knew he loved us, and he knew we loved him.

I never saw Papá just lounge around. When he was tired, he stretched out on his sofa in the library and took a catnap. When he was worried or had to think things over, he paced back and forth in the living room, but he never burdened us children with his personal concerns. Papá had Mamá as well as good friends with whom to talk things over. He was from the old school where fathers did not communicate with their children about finances or personal matters. As the father of a large family, Papá took his family responsibilities seriously.

He was also conscientious concerning his military responsibilities. Our father was a hero in the Austrian Navy, but Papá was not the first in our family to serve in the navy. Our grandfather, August Johann Trapp, was born in Germany, but he became an Austrian citizen, joined the Austrian Navy, and was stationed in Zara, a small Austrian harbor on the Dalmatian coast. Papá told us that our grandfather was appointed commander of the SMS *Saida* and was cruising in the Mediterranean, west of Italy, when a violent storm threatened the ship and crew. By his keen maneuvers, he was able to steer the vessel onto a sandbank and to save the crew single-handedly. For this heroic rescue, he was awarded the Iron Cross, Third Class, and was elevated to knighthood by Franz Joseph I, emperor of Austria. From that day—November 18, 1876—our grandfather's name was August Johann Ritter von Trapp.[1]

His son, my father, Georg, was born in Zara on April 4, 1880. Georg inherited his father's title and later followed in his father's footsteps by joining the Austrian Navy. When Papá was a very young child, his father died of typhoid fever, and his mother, my grandmother, Hedwig Wepler von Trapp, moved with her three children—Hede, Georg, and Werner—to Pola.[2] There my grandmother made sure that her children went to a Lutheran elementary school, according to her and her husband's faith. As an officer's widow, my grandmother received a small pension to support herself and her children. It did not provide for an extravagant lifestyle, but it enabled the family to survive at a time when the social order did not allow someone in my grandmother's position to seek employment. In those days an inheritance was very important to a woman, especially when she was a widow with young children. Later, when her sons had careers, they helped her financially, but their salaries were not large enough to permit them to send very much to their mother.

At the age of fourteen, Georg von Trapp entered the naval academy in Fiume.[3] Toward the end of a rigorous training period, he and his classmates were assigned to a sailing ship, the SMS *Saida II*, to complete their training. Ironically Georg was assigned to a ship with the same name as the ship that his father had previously commanded. Having no single destination, the ship was to sail around the world with the newly trained cadets. The trip was scheduled to take the crew through the Suez Canal, heading east through the Indian Ocean to Australia. There the SMS *Saida II* was welcomed with open arms, and the cadets and officers were entertained as honored guests. The Austrian emperor even granted an extension of their visit, at the request of their captain. In his description of this trip, Papá mentioned the Marquesas Islands as being especially beautiful. These islands impressed him to such an extent that he always dreamed of going back to them at some future time.

The journey of the SMS *Saida II* came to an early end, however. Signs of unrest and hostilities by thousands of followers of a secret society, known as the Boxers, against missionaries and other foreigners in China caused great concern among Western nations.

These nations then sent ships to China to monitor the situation, watching for serious actions that the Boxers might take against their embassies and the quarters where Westerners lived.[4] Because of the perilous state of affairs, the captain of the SMS *Saida II* received a telegram on June 9, 1899, ordering the ship with the cadets to return home. At that time she was sailing north along the coast of China as far as Shanghai.

From Woosung Harbor, Cadet von Trapp wrote to his mother in Pola:

> Hurrah, this moment we received a telegram that we are going home! On board one sees only happy faces. Our route goes back via Hong Kong, Batavia [now Jakarta, Indonesia], Port Mahi [on the Seychelles], Aden, then back to Pola. We shall arrive in Pola most likely the middle or end of October. By then you will already have more accurate dates.
>
> Your faithful Son,
> Georg

Cadet von Trapp did not see much of his mother when he reached Pola. After a short furlough, he was assigned to the navigation staff of the Austrian cruiser SMS *Zenta*, on an operational mission to China where the Boxer Rebellion was increasing in intensity.[5] Thus, Cadet von Trapp had the opportunity to get a firsthand education in the field of navigation, working side by side with those most experienced in this field.

The SMS *Zenta* had instructions to proceed to the harbor of Shanghai. After passing through the Strait of Formosa, the ship encountered threatening weather; it had entered the zone of heavy typhoons. The *Zenta* had already braved several storms on the way, but this one was a full-blown typhoon. Its raging waters had swallowed several steamships and Chinese junks. The little cruiser, however, survived the height of the storm with very little damage and finally arrived, many hours late, in Shanghai. There the ship and the

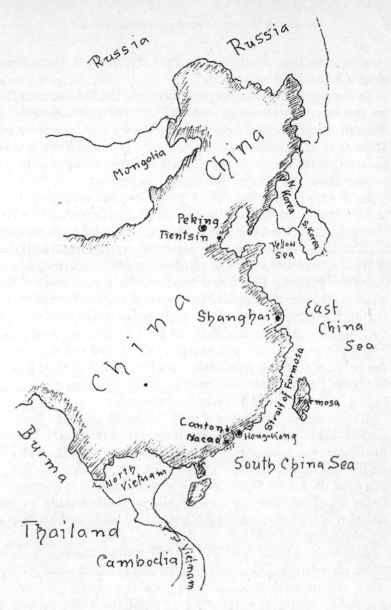

The Coast of China circa 1900

crew were welcomed with salutes from the other Western ships already anchored in the harbor.

As I write about this part of my father's trip to China, it occurs to me that he could have easily lost his life in order to help save the Western population there from sure death. There would have been no Trapp Family, no Trapp Family Singers, no *Sound of Music*, if God had not held His hand over this little cruiser to prevent it from being overwhelmed by the raging sea during this typhoon.

In Shanghai the captain of the SMS *Zenta* followed his orders, transmitted via the Austrian consul, to continue immediately north after loading coal and provisions. Their course took them through the China Sea and the Yellow Sea. Along the way the captain and crew of the *Zenta* received news of terrible atrocities occurring in the vicinity of Nanking. Consulting together, the commanders of the Western ships decided to sail to the harbor of Tientsin to be closer to Peking. There the attack upon the Western quarters began just when the ships arrived. The international force of English, American, French, German, Italian, and Austrian soldiers and sailors stormed the forts and freed the inhabitants in a fierce hand-to-hand battle. Georg von Trapp and his detachment excelled in this encounter, and he was later decorated for bravery and promoted.

The things that Papá saw during the battle in China were so terrible that he never told us about them. I later read a report about this conflict in a newspaper (*Neue Illustrierte Wochenschau* of May 1, 1960). This newspaper article, "Sixty Years Ago: Boxer Rebellion," described the horror of the Boxer War and featured the heroism of Georg von Trapp and his crew. Published posthumously on the occasion of my father's eightieth birthday, it recounted his rescue actions during the rebellion.

Papá told us a humorous story of a happening in the mountains of China where his detail was sent for a few days of rest. It was very cold, and they were accommodated in an inn with no heat. To make his guests comfortable, at least during the night, the landlord provided hot water bottles. These were placed in the foot of the beds under the blankets before the guests retired for the evening. There were no electric lights in the inn; the guests had to use oil lamps.

During the first night after everyone had retired, a strange noise came from one room. Alarmed, some of the crew went toward the noisy room. Lantern in hand, they opened the door. What did they find? One of the officers was hitting his bed frantically with a stick while a swinging lamp, suspended from the ceiling, was hitting him on the head.

He had gone to bed in the dark, unaware that he would find a "warm friend" under his blankets. When he stretched out, his feet felt the warmth of the hot water bottle, but he thought it was an animal, perhaps a rat. He jumped out of bed and went for his walking stick to drive the imagined animal out of his bed. He must have felt pretty silly when he discovered that he had been frightened stiff by a hot water bottle and a lampshade!

On the way back from the Orient, the SMS *Zenta* made a stop in the Holy Land. Papá was fortunate to have a private guide, a kind Franciscan padre, who gave Papá a tour of the holy places and showed him where to buy souvenirs. Among other things, Papá bought many clear glass bottles of Jordan water embossed on one side with the words *Jordan Water* and on the opposite side with a cross. Perhaps he had in mind that someday he would have a big family, and Jordan water would be a special way to have his children baptized.

Smyrna (Izmir), Turkey, was another stop where the crew was able to go ashore. This town's specialty was its handmade carpets. The shopkeepers' entertainment was to see whether the customers were smart enough to barter the carpet down to an acceptable price. I do not know how Papá rated in their estimation, but he bought some beautiful carpets in Turkey that later adorned our home.

One souvenir from his trips to China that always intrigued me was a wood block with Chinese characters carved into it. In the early 1950s, when we gave concerts in Hawaii, a professor from the University of Hawaii translated the words on the block for me. It was a house blessing that read: "A Thousand Blessings Be Upon You."

When the SMS *Zenta* arrived back in Pola at the end of the mission to China, a great welcome awaited her brave crew.

Istria

1914 ~ to ~ 1918

Trieste

Fiume

Pola

Lussin-Grande

Lussin-Piccolo

THE · ADRIATIC · SEA

After his first military adventure, the next great event in Papá's life was his marriage to my mother. It is a story that Edwyn Gray, an English writer on marine subjects and the invention of the torpedo, describes in part in his book, *The Devil's Device*.[6] He mentions that Papá met and married Agathe Whitehead, the granddaughter of the torpedo's inventor, Robert Whitehead, an Englishman.

In 1908 the naval authorities sent Georg von Trapp to Fiume to study firsthand the construction of submarines and torpedoes. When one of the first submarines constructed in the Whitehead factory, the U-5, was launched in 1909, Agathe Whitehead was asked to perform the ceremony. At that occasion, Georg von Trapp was standing next to her on the flag-bedecked platform, unaware that he would be assigned to command this very submarine, and that she who launched the vessel would one day become his wife. This story is told in detail in the next chapter.

Two years later, on January 14, 1911, Georg and Agathe were married, and Georg's mother, Hedwig Wepler von Trapp, was able to attend the wedding in spite of the fact that she was not well. In October of the same year, she died of consumption at the age of fifty-six. Georg's brother, Werner, wrote the following letter to his grandmother, Engeline Wepler, and his Aunt Minna, in which he mentioned the arrival of the firstborn to Georg and Agathe, a little boy named Rupert:

November 11, 1911

Dear Nona and Aunt Minna,

Thank you both from the bottom of my heart for your kind and loving words, which Aunt Minna wrote to me.

Of course you knew Mother well, but did you know her as a mother? Did you know what a childhood paradise she created for us?

I remember Mother as so loving, so good, so friendly and gentle, yet so strong and proud. But the greatest was her love, the love for us children. She dedicated her whole life to us, even her health. She lived only for us and the memory of our father. In her boundless humility and selflessness she seemed to say, "Now that my children have entered their life's careers, I have done my duty; now I want to rest and go to Father."

Now she is with him and our parents have their quiet little house and they look down on us and protect us.

Poor loving Mother, now at last, that her children could care for her, she goes away.

Georg must have written to you about her last days. Until about ten days before she died I was with her, but then I had to leave. When we said good-bye we both knew—it was for the last time.

Mother had a gentle, peaceful end; she went to sleep. This was the only thing I could have wished for her. When I came back there, she lay so quietly and peacefully, so loving as always. She kept her lovely expression until the end when Georg and I closed the coffin. For this we were alone.

Now finally she is free from her sufferings and the worries of life. However she lives on in us; and how good it is to know that there is a Wiedersehen [we'll see each other again]. That helps.

Next year I would like to come, but everything is so uncertain about my military service.

I guess by now you know that a little boy "appeared" at Georg's. Mother would have liked to live to see him—she was so sad that she was not able anymore to sew something for him, but she did crochet a little jacket.

It occurs to me now, that I am alone in the evenings.

May God bless you, adieu. I thank you from my heart and greet you as

Your faithful grandson and nephew,
Werner

A large home was built for the young family of Georg von Trapp to become known as Villa Trapp.[7] It was situated outside Pola, where Papá was stationed, near the shore on a hill called "Monte Paradiso" with a magnificent view of the Adriatic Sea. The house was built in the native style of the region and big enough for a large family. However, it was not to be the home of Georg von Trapp's family for long.

In 1914, a year after my arrival, the First World War began, and the area along the seashore was evacuated. All civilians had to retire to a safer place in the interior of the country. Our mother and her two children—my brother Rupert and I—were invited by her mother to stay in the Erlhof for the duration of the war. The Erlhof, our grandmother's scenic mountain chalet, was situated on the shore of Austria's Zeller Lake in the Alps.

Papá was given the command of one of the first submarines in the Austrian Navy. The submarine was still in its experimental stages but was pressed into service at the sudden start of World War I. In his book, Edwyn Gray writes,

> Georg's appointment to the Whitehead factory came to an end in due time, and he was sent off to command Torpedo-boat 52 where he quickly demonstrated his professional ability. He stood high in the esteem of his senior officers and it was apparent that, barring accidents, the young Lieutenant was destined for a top place in the Imperial Navy. To give him further experience, the Admiralty appointed him as captain of the submarine U-5—the boat which his wife had launched before their marriage.

Papá's experience on the SMS *Saida II* as well as the rescue action on behalf of the Austrian embassy in China may have awakened in him a spirit of adventure. His willingness to take risks, however, was moderated by his excellent judgment and outstanding presence of mind. Without these two traits, Papá could not have been successful as the commander of his submarine, the U-5.

His most daring move at the beginning of World War I was an underwater torpedo launch at the French battleship *Leon Gambetta* by night with the rising full moon as a background. It was a one-time opportunity. He took it and succeeded in sinking the ship.

In this particular episode, which occurred on April 27, 1915, Georg von Trapp took a double risk in a maneuver that was beyond the call of duty. If he failed and came back safely, he would have been

court-martialed because he maneuvered outside his assigned territory. If he failed and was destroyed by the battleship, he would have lost his own life, the lives of the crew and the submarine.

However risky this maneuver was, the risk was modified by his carefully considered tactics and his full trust in his crew who, in turn, fully trusted him. The *Leon Gambetta* disappeared in the waves within nine minutes. From the day of the loss of the *Leon Gambetta*, the enemy refrained from sending more battleships into that area of the Mediterranean; it was assumed that Austria had a far superior submarine fleet than actually was the case. Instantly Georg von Trapp became a hero by the standards of the Austrian Navy and an imaginary threat to the enemy. This heroic maneuver at the beginning of the war earned him the Maria Theresian Cross, the highest award possible in the Austrian Navy. The title of baron also came with the award. Papá would later write a book about his experiences in World War I.[8]

When the news of his extraordinary accomplishment reached the mainland, Georg von Trapp was considered a hero by the civilian population. Schoolgirls sent him congratulatory letters, and postcards were printed with his photograph and that of the U-5. For him, his naval victory was bittersweet. He thought of the men and officers who went down with their ship. His only consolation was that he helped his country in its fight for survival.

Yes, Georg von Trapp was a hero, but to us, he was our Papá. When he came home on furlough, Papá came back to a family that was very proud of him. I remember the excitement of those days. I cannot recall how often he came home, but I do know that his visits were quite frequent. Life on the submarine was extremely nerve-wracking because of the cramped conditions, the fumes, and the lack of oxygen. Therefore, frequent rest periods on land were mandatory for the officers and crew.

During that time, Rupert and I did not understand exactly what the war was all about, but we did understand that Papá went out on a ship that could dive underwater to shoot at the enemy. He sank those enemy ships and then came home to see us. When he arrived at the Erlhof, he laid away his navy uniform and put on civilian clothes. After a good night's rest, Papá loved to play with us. Early in the morning, we knocked on his door and sang our self-invented songs for him.

He often "became" an elephant, allowing us to ride on his back. Sometimes Papá would tell us stories to make us laugh and shiver— stories he invented about dragons, giants, and all sorts of exciting things. Once in the middle of a story, I asked him, "Is this a true story?" He answered truthfully, "No, it is not true." I asked, "Why, then, do you tell it to us?" With this question the story ended, and I didn't hear another story for quite a while.

Another time Papá pulled a matchbox from his pocket and laid some matches out on the table. He pointed and said, "This is my submarine, and these are the enemy ships." Then he explained to us about his sea battles. We could not fully understand all this, but we did realize that our father was in danger and could get hurt in the war.

We let our imaginations run freely. We made him lie down on the large sofa in the living room and told him that he had a very big wound on his head. I was the nurse and I tied up the wound with his big white handkerchief, and Rupert, the doctor, felt his pulse and prescribed bed rest. This seemed a welcome order to Papá, and he promptly fell asleep.

In the mornings, Rupert and I would often go to his door and knock. After we heard him say, "Herein" (come in), we ran in, jumped on his bed, and said, "Good morning, Papá." Then he picked us up, one by one, and placed us on his knees, with his legs stretched out. As he slowly bent his knees, making a mountain, we rose to the top to be suddenly dropped into a deep valley. We would take this ride into the air again and again, never tiring of the game. In this environment, he could forget the war for the moment and be the loving father he really was.

In *The Sound of Music*, the Captain was portrayed as stern, distant, and unyielding. In reality the Captain, our father, was gentle, kind, and sensitive. Mamá could not have found a better father for us.

2

Mamá, Our Sunshine

Our mamá, Agathe Whitehead von Trapp, was a gentle beauty, calm, natural, and quietly effective. My earliest memory is of her wearing a reddish-brown ankle-length skirt with a white blouse trimmed in red Hungarian embroidery around the neckline, shoulders, and wrists. The blouse was most becoming on her. Once I watched her put up her hair, creating an immaculate hairdo. She combed her brown waves up, wound her long hair into a loose bun on top of her head, and pinned it in place. Then she heated a curling iron over a small flame and curled the ends of her hair in the back and around the sides of her face. To a little girl, this was an extraordinary event because we children did not usually see our mother until she was completely dressed and ready for her day. I admired her greatly.

Mamá was able to run a big household with a cook, maids, and other staff members in a quiet and gentle manner. Every person who knew Mamá loved her and remembered her for years, including the staff. She never said a harsh word. She said what had to be said in a kind, but firm, voice. When she entered the room, it seemed that the sun was rising. I am not surprised that for Papá, it was love at first sight.

Mamá was born in Fiume on June 14, 1890, to John and Agathe Whitehead, and she was one of six children: John, Frank, Agathe,[1] Mary, Robert, and Joan. In her parents' home, the Villa Whitehead,

Mamá received an aristocratic upbringing. The household included a large staff. Private tutors and a live-in piano teacher provided Mamá's education.

Papá told me the story of how he first met Mamá at a party after the launching of the submarine U-5 in 1909. He was one of the invited guests at a social event arranged by Countess Alice Hoyos, Robert Whitehead's daughter and Agathe's aunt, to be held following the ceremony. After studying and working all week at the factory, young Georg must have been ready to dress up and go to a party. In those days, any of the guests who were able to perform music were asked to provide the entertainment. Mother Whitehead played the piano very well. She and her daughter Agathe, who played the violin, entertained the guests with their music that very evening.

Georg also came from a musical family. His father frequently attended the opera in Zara, and after returning home, he would sit at the piano and play some of the music he had just heard. Georg himself played the violin, the guitar, and the mandolin. At the party, he was delighted with the music he heard, but he also was impressed with Agathe. As she played the violin, he noticed her beauty and calm spirit. At nineteen she was not only beautiful but also mature and self-assured. Later he would tell me that on this evening he knew she was meant for him.

That night they danced, and Agathe's mother invited Georg for afternoon tea with the family at their villa in Fiume. Eventually Georg was invited to visit at the Whiteheads' summer home, the Erlhof. Not far from the house, a brook came down the steep mountainside.

I remember a day when I was about seven years old and Papá took me for a walk near this brook. He was wearing an olive green suit, which I liked very much. He confided in me that this suit was very special to him because he had worn it when he proposed to Mamá. We continued up a little footpath that ran alongside the brook. My father showed me a huge boulder with a clean, flat surface, which stood next to the path. This boulder must have come down from the mountain during the Ice Age. Its rounded edges told the story.

On this rock, Papá and Mamá talked things over and pledged their lives to each other. Soon after this, their engagement was announced. Since Agathe was only nineteen years old, Mother Whitehead suggested that they wait to be married until her daughter was of age. They waited two years. Georg von Trapp and Agathe Whitehead were married in a fairy-tale wedding in Fiume on January 14, 1911.

I recently received a description of this event from the archives in Graz, Austria, that had been written at the time of the wedding by my maternal grandmother, my uncle Franky, and another relative, Margit Kinsky. Written in German, it was a wedding souvenir for the guests. According to this booklet, the wedding festivities took place over a period of three days. My grandmother knew how to organize very well. She was sending her oldest daughter into the world, and it was to be the most wonderful day of her life. Relatives were invited from England, Germany, and Austria. They came by ship across the English Channel and by train from everywhere else. Accommodations had been arranged in the town of Fiume for all the guests.

Papá's mother, aunt, and grandmother arrived from Pola on January 12. The only function that day was the civil registration for the marriage license.

All the other guests arrived the next day. The harbor was teeming with little boats, known as *Barkassen*, taking the guests from the train station to the town of Fiume, where the Villa Whitehead was prepared for the wedding festivities. There was great joy and excitement as the guests were greeted. Tea was served at 4:00 p.m. Of course, the trousseau and the many wedding gifts were laid out for all to see.

An administrative official came from the torpedo factory of the bride's grandfather to congratulate the bride with a cordial address and to present her with a lovely silver jardiniere, or planter. Next, the foreman of the factory workers gave a lovely and meaningful speech to Mamá and brought a beautiful floral arrangement. My grandmother noted that these presentations were for her and her children, a very touching proof of the affection and loyalty shown by the factory staff for the Whitehead family. I am sure that Mamá's father was greatly missed by his family at this significant event; he had died in 1902.

On the evening of January 13, a delicious buffet was set up in the dining room, and everyone was in high spirits. A party was scheduled for nine o'clock with music and dancing. Twelve members of the navy band, who were selected to entertain with dance music, were placed in the front of the ballroom. Grandmother mentioned that they played as well as the best Viennese band, which is the highest praise any Austrian can give to a band.

The guests were dressed in gala attire. My grandmother, the mother of the bride, wore a white evening dress with a train, a long veil of Venetian lace, and exquisite jewelry. For this affair, the bride-to-be wore a dress of light blue brocade with a train, a diamond tiara (a wedding present from her two older brothers), a diamond brooch, and a pearl necklace. She and the bridegroom in his formal uniform were the most outstanding pair on the dance floor.

All the guests were present, including the representatives from the torpedo factory and many friends from Fiume. The soiree ended at midnight since the wedding was the next day.

During breakfast on the fourteenth, the day of the wedding, a detail of Georg's submarine crew arrived with a beautiful floral arrangement. Many more flowers and congratulatory notes were delivered for the bride. Grandmother wrote that at 11:00 a.m. the wedding guests assembled at the Austrian Naval Academy. The superintendent of the academy, Captain Schubert, had graciously placed the chapel and the public rooms at the family's disposal.

Grandmother added that the guests arrived in horse-drawn carriages and wagons of all kinds. The bride and her mother were the last ones to appear at the church. On the way to the church, as they passed the houses of the workers, women and children lined the sidewalks, waving and filling the air with their shouts of joy. Many people from the academy were already assembled outside the church.

My grandmother noted that Agathe looked so young and sweet in her bridal gown and veil. She was calm, natural, and simple.

As the guests entered the church two by two, the organ was played by the multitalented cello teacher of the bride's brother. The teacher had traveled to Fiume just for this occasion. The bride's religion teacher, a priest, gave a moving address and performed the wedding ceremony. After the ceremony, the chaplain of the naval academy offered the Wedding Mass. It was truly a solemn celebration that proceeded flawlessly. The bride and bridegroom were a radiant pair.

Georg and Agathe were the first to leave the church. They were met with shouts of congratulations and jubilation. The crew of Georg's submarine, along with the factory workers, had adorned the pathway from the church entrance to the main road with flagpoles, decorated with garlands of greenery and flowers. British and Austrian flags were flown as well as the coats of arms of both families. The people stood in line on both sides of the garden path, waving their hands and hats. They gesticulated, as only Italians can, and shouted, "Eviva I Sposi!" (Long live the newlyweds!). Grandmother wrote that it was especially touching because the members of the submarine crew and the factory workers had planned and executed this ovation for their commander and his young wife on their own.

Agathe and Georg thanked them, greatly moved by their outburst of affection. The workers and sailors followed them to the villa to get another glimpse of the pair. As the couple went up the steps to be with the family for lunch, they turned and waved to all the enthusiastic well-wishers.

In the living room, the whole family congratulated the young couple. Georg and Agathe were then seated at the center of the head table with honored guests on either side. Tables were set for the wedding party and other guests to the right and left of the head table. Each table was richly decorated with flowers; the silver jardiniere adorned the head table. Two lovely floral arrangements, in the form of sailing ships, were presented to the married couple. Delightful speeches were given, and the general atmosphere was joyful.

It was agreed upon that the newlyweds would leave without a formal farewell. Immediately after black coffee was served, the mothers of the bride and groom went to the bedroom where Agathe changed for her honeymoon trip. When it was time to depart, the two mothers accompanied their children downstairs. On the staircase, they were greeted again with the shouts of well-wishers and congratulations from all the wedding guests.

Agathe's brother John had asked for the pleasure of taking the pair to the train station. After many thanks and good-byes, they got into the car, which was decorated with garlands of greenery and flowers. Since they were going to Metuglie,[2] they had to pass by the entrance of the villa a second time and were showered again with flowers, blessings, and good wishes. According to Grandmother, they could not have had a more beautiful, harmonious, and joyful wedding.

After reading this account of my parents' wedding, I think I can detect a secret tear running down Grandmother's cheek as she accompanied her beloved Agathe down the stairs to the entrance to say a last good-bye to her. She had poured her love for her daughter into this wedding, and now she would not see her any longer because the couple was going to live in Pola where Georg was stationed. Little did she know that three years later, her daughter would be back, along with her two small children, because of circumstances beyond anyone's control.

The rumblings of World War I started in June 1914, and all civilians who lived near the coast had to leave areas designated as war zones. Grandmother Whitehead owned a large summer home in the interior of Austria, the Erlhof. That year she invited Mamá to come there with her two children for the duration of the war while Papá was away in the service. Rupert was two and a half, and I was fifteen months old. Therefore, my first memories are of my grandmother's house, the Erlhof.

Looking back, I think it must have been a great hardship for Mamá to give up her new and beautiful home in Pola, to be separated from her husband, and to endure the uncertainties of World War I with her two small children. But instead of mourning, she was busy around the Erlhof, joining her mother and sisters, Mary and Joan, in the activities of daily life.

Mamá could knit, crochet, and sew. I remember her sitting on the bench in front of the Erlhof, knitting woolen stockings for the soldiers at the front, making bandages of woolen material for leggings, and even white bandages for the wounded.

Not only could Mamá sew well, but she also taught me how to sew when I was four years old. We sewed by hand then, not with a sewing machine. I learned to make small hemstitches, and now every time I hem a skirt I think of those precious moments when she taught me these stitches. I wanted to learn to sew as she did and did not mind practicing the small stitches for what seemed to me to be hours. Mamá made my dresses, underwear, and even a coat. It was made of a bluish gray material that I thought was beautiful. I could not wait until I could wear it!

Mamá knew how to knit and crochet very well and very quickly. She was able to knit and read at the same time, an achievement I admired but never could accomplish. She did this with her book in her lap without looking at what she was knitting or crocheting. When I asked her to teach me how to knit and crochet, she did. In later years, my sister Maria and I sat for hours knitting woolen knee-highs for Papá. He wore them often, even though they were a bit too long on the top.

Mamá, her sister Mary (Tante Mary to us), and Tante Connie, the wife of Papá's brother, Werner, worked together to make knee-high snow boots for us. For the boots themselves, they used heavy ivory-colored felt, and for the soles, they used some brown carpetlike material. They must have taken the design from the boots worn by the Bosnian soldiers who were stationed at Grandmother's farm.[3] The soldiers helped the farmer with his work, and in the evening, they sat outside the farmhouse singing their native songs. We learned one of these songs not from the soldiers , but from Tante Mary and Tante Joan, who had learned it from the soldiers.

The song sounded something like this: "Milke moye moye moye, Milke moye moye moye, Milke moye lasemta lasemta." We sang this song with great enthusiasm because of its lively melody, although we did not understand the words. Sometimes Mamá and her two sisters would sing other simple folk songs in two parts, which we children quickly learned and sang among ourselves. Mamá was very musical. Not only did she sing beautifully, but she also played the piano and the violin.

I learned so much from Mamá during those World War I days just by being with her and watching her. She planted flowers and vegetables. Mamá made a garden just for me and showed me how to plant the seeds. Many of the activities that are still useful to me, such as gardening and sewing, I learned from Mamá during those days.

On Sundays, Mamá and the aunts would row us across the lake to go to Mass in the thirteenth-century church in the town of Zell am See. I would sit in the stern of the boat, watching them row while trying not to get seasick until we arrived at the little pier. There the boat was tied up until it was time to row back.

After Mass, Mamá would take us across the village square to the fruit stand of Frau Steinwender. I can still see her friendly face, like a rosy-cheeked apple, with an unforgettable smile as she greeted Mamá and said to us, "Ja, die lieben Kinder" (Oh, the dear children). Then Mamá would buy some fruit, and Frau Steinwender would make a small cone of white paper and fill it with cherries or some other small fruit in season, such as plums or apricots, for each of us. She had loved Mamá for a very long time because she had seen her for many a Sunday, even before we were born. Frau Steinwender wore her white hair in a braid around her head, and her face shone like a sunflower. She must have been well into her seventies.

Then Mamá would go into the bank building next door to visit Frau von Lammer, the owner of the bank. Sometimes she would go upstairs to visit the wife of one of Papá's officers who lived in an apartment with her little son, Stutz von Jedina, who later became our playmate. Frau von Jedina was a tall, thin lady, and very friendly to us, but to me, she always seemed sad. In the apartment next to Frau von Jedina lived Frau von Kastner, yet another wife of an officer in the Austrian Navy.

By then it was time to take the crossing back to our grandmother's house on Zeller Lake, which was always peaceful and blue on those excursions. The majestic mountains hovered protectively around us.

Every night Mamá would come to our beds to say evening prayers with us, which included a prayer for Papá, who was out at sea to defend our coastlines. There near the shore of the Adriatic Sea stood our house. We prayed for our father and our house. God graciously protected both.

During the war years at the Erlhof, colds and coughs were common occurrences. In such cases Mamá would put us to bed with a hot, wet compress all around our upper bodies. These compresses were called *Wickel* (wrappings). In a darkened room, we were supposed to sweat and were told to try to sleep while waiting it out. A hot cup of linden blossom tea with honey completed the treatment. The honey definitely sweetened it for us. It tasted wonderful.

Three-quarters of an hour later, Mamá would return to unwrap the compresses and dry us. She then would give us clean nightgowns, after which we would get a glass of cold water. I can still recall the relief after the unwrapping! Sweating was considered to be the remedy for respiratory infections. It was usually very effective.

Living in such an isolated place as the Erlhof, we regarded anything that broke the routine of daily life as a major event. There was excitement when the first berries ripened, and when we discovered ducks on the lake. Everybody had to come and take a look as the ducks dove and disappeared! We wondered where they would come out of the water. Oh! They came out so far away from where they dove!

Another event was the coming and going of the trains. We watched the trains pulling into the station at Zell am See across the lake. Sometimes they brought guests who dropped in to visit.

The greatest excitement, however, was the arrival of a new baby. In our time, the "stork" brought babies, and because they always seemed to arrive in the morning, it was natural that they were in bed with Mamá. Four von Trapp children were born at the Erlhof: Maria, Werner, Hedwig, and Johanna.

In September 1914, when Maria was born, the navy did not permit personnel to send or receive private messages. So the only way Mamá could announce the birth of the new baby to Papá was to send an official-sounding telegram to Captain von Trapp: "S.M.S. Marie eingelaufen" (S.M.S. Marie arrived). The telegram was delivered without difficulty.

Christmas of 1914 was the year when Papá's brother, Uncle Werner, was on leave for the holy season. I was not quite two years old then, but I remember his visit distinctly. Uncle Werner was killed in action in May of 1915. My brother Werner, born on December 21, 1915, was named in memory of him. Two more sisters followed Werner. Hedwig arrived in July of 1917 and then Johanna in 1919, after the end of the war. Later, still another baby sister would arrive.

I have a beautiful memory of those days. Papá and Mamá were sitting next to each other in the living room at the Erlhof and talking quietly. As young as I was, it left an indelible impression on me. Today, I can still see the picture of my parents as clearly as I saw it then. I felt the peace and unity that existed between them, and I thought, *This is how it is when one is married.* Only later in life did I find out that this is very rare.

In spite of the terrible war, our early years were happy and peaceful, entirely due to the atmosphere created by our mother and grandmother. Mamá, with her shining personality, her musical talent, her love of nature, her faith, her kindness, and most of all her devotion to her family, gave us the gift of a wonderful childhood and laid the foundation for our later years. Those happy times took place at our grandmother's home.

3

Life with Gromi

ぞぐ♡ざぐ

O ur maternal grandmother, Agathe Breuner Whitehead, was
unique. Living at her summer home, the Erlhof, as I did, I
learned to know her well. My brothers and sisters and I called
her "Gromi." As a small child, my brother Rupert invented this name
because he could not pronounce *Grossmutter* (grandmother).

Gromi, born in 1856, was the daughter of Count August Breuner.
Thus, she was Austrian aristocracy. She was wise enough, however,
to know that social standing is not everything, so when she fell in love
with a "commoner"—and an Englishman besides—she married
him. John Whitehead was an engineer; he inherited his father's
talent for engineering and became his father's partner in the torpedo
factory, which was located in Fiume. There Gromi and Grandfather
made their home, the Villa Whitehead, across the street from the
factory.

I did not know my grandfather, John Whitehead, for he died in
1902, nine years before my parents' marriage. Gromi never spoke of
him to us. I believe she grieved all her life and was just not up to
talking about her husband. I only remember Gromi as a widow.

Gromi was a short, rather stout, dignified woman, and she had
very good posture. She wore only the colors of light gray or beige in
the summer and black or charcoal gray in the winter. The white veil
on top of her hairdo, traditional for English widows of that time,

25

enhanced her suits and added to her dignity. It was very becoming, and I could not imagine her without it. I cannot say that Gromi was beautiful, but she had a natural charm and was totally unaffected. She was who she was and did not try to be more.

Because Gromi was rather heavy, she went to Karlsbad, a spa in Bohemia, now the Czech Republic, to take "the cure" (a reducing diet). She would bring home a treat known as *Karlsbader Oblaten*, which was a specialty of the Karlsbad spa. It consisted of two large, paper-thin wafers with a sugary layer in between. This treat came in a round tin box with a thin sheet of paper between each one. It was so delicious.

For the journey to Karlsbad, she took along tightly packed suitcases. I believe packing a suitcase was a special challenge for Gromi; when confronted by a suitcase, she must have had a puzzle in mind. To her, this meant do not leave any—no, not even the slightest—space between the objects to be packed and make sure that they fit snugly into each other, always wrapped in white tissue paper. The result of this kind of packing was a suitcase as heavy as a rock. She was very proud of her packing, and she taught it to me. It never seemed to occur to her that the suitcases could have been too heavy for the men who carried them. But then again, did anyone ever tell her so? How could she have known? Men are stronger than old ladies are, and the ones who carried her suitcases never seemed to complain!

After Gromi's husband, John, died, she bought a piece of land for a summer home located in the Austrian Alps on the Zeller Lake. On the property was a farmhouse with stables. A local farmer worked the farm and later supplied the family with meat, poultry, eggs, and milk. The farm was called "Der Alte Erlhof" (the Old Erlhof).

This beautiful spot in the mountains was an isolated area. A country dirt road ran around the lake, bordered on either side by a wooden fence. This road divided Gromi's property: the farm buildings stood at the foot of a mountain, and on the lakeside was a stony field, where she decided to build. Across the lake, Gromi could see the lovely view of the snow-clad mountains, the Kitzsteinhorn, and the adjacent mountain ranges. With the help of a local architect, Gromi turned the stony field into a little paradise.

She herself told me how she did it. She knew how she wanted the house built and all that was connected with it. The architect drew the plans according to her description. When she had a special idea that he would object to on the grounds that it was not possible, she would show him how it *could* be done.

On this piece of property, she created an almost self-sufficient unit. There was the farm with livestock, milk cows, chickens, and pigs. Below the road by the lake was the house for her family, a chalet built of masonry and wood with a granite foundation. There was a smaller building in the same style, housing the kitchen and the servants' dining room and sleeping quarters. A closed-in corridor with glass windows and a glass door on each side connected the two buildings, making a convenient walkway from kitchen to dining room and yard to garden. There was also an underground icehouse for refrigeration. In a small building in back of the main house three women did the daily laundry for everyone on the premises.

Gromi built another smaller house for the gardener and his family. He took care of the vegetable garden and tended the plantings around the house and grounds; he planted trees and flower beds, according to Gromi's directions.

In the garden was a small house with a bench inside. It had an unusual construction. The roof was solid wood, but the sides were made of wooden poles with spaces between them. The poles were overgrown with a vine, *Pfeifenstrauch* (pipe bush), thus forming a trellis. Its huge leaves were heart shaped, and the blossoms looked like little pipes. We picked them and pretended we were smoking.

On the lakeshore, below the house, were two boathouses. One was for the flatboats, a local type of boat in which one had to row in standing position, used solely by the staff. The second boathouse was for the two rowboats, imported from London, which were used by the family. There was also a wooden barrack on what was formerly a tennis court, which served as storage and occasionally as a play area for the children.

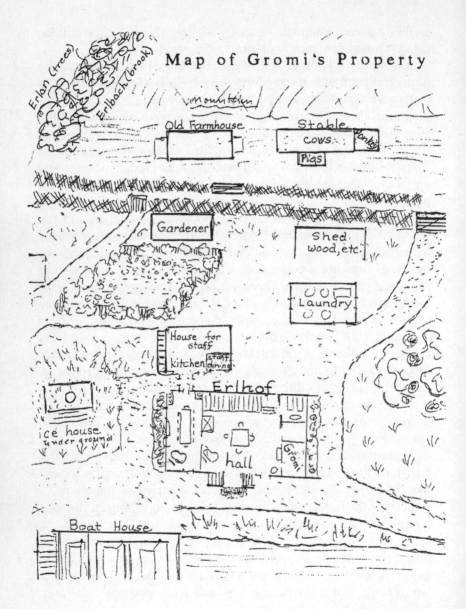

Map of Gromi's Property

Erlen (trees)
Erlbach (brook)

mountain

Old Farmhouse

Stable

cows

donkey

Pigs

Gardener

Shed
wood, etc.

Laundry

House for
staff

kitchen

staff
dining

ice house
under ground

Erlhof

hall

Gromi

Boat House

A mountain stream bordered Gromi's property on one side. At times it was a little brook, but during long periods of rainy weather, it swelled to a rushing mountain stream. Then it brought stones and tree trunks as well as boulders down from the mountainside. The name of the brook was Erlbach because of the trees, *die Erlen,* which grew on its banks. This brook started to form a peninsula because it deposited an enormous amount of debris into the lake. The rock in this area is slate, which is one of the oldest rock formations and is very brittle.

On the other side of this mountain brook was another little building, a playhouse for Gromi's youngest daughter, Joan. It was a wooden hut with a bench and a built-in table. There was a narrow bridge leading to it.

All of this was built at the turn of the twentieth century when Gromi's children were young and needed a place to spend their summers away from the heat of the city. When we came along in 1914, the Erlhof was simply there, and we did not realize until much later how Gromi had developed this beautiful summer home for her children.

When my mother moved back to the Erlhof, she brought her two children and a nanny who had been with her since my brother Rupert's birth. In addition to taking in my mother and her two children, Gromi generously invited Tante Connie, the widow of my father's brother, Werner, and her child.

Since Tante Connie was Irish and knew only a little German, Gromi and her family spoke English most of the time. Therefore, in our early childhood, Rupert and I learned German and English. As strange as it may sound, I believe God saw to it that we acquired, at an early age, the knowledge and the feeling for the very language we would need in what would eventually become our home, America.

Our nanny was very important in our lives. Her name was Marie Holzinger, but we called her "Nenni," a germanization of *Nanny.* Nenni spoke only German, the Austrian variety, of course. She was a very kind person and was Mamá's right hand. Nenni kept the nursery in order and provided a daily routine for us. She gave us meals, made sure we had an afternoon nap, took us for walks in the garden, watched over us while we played, bathed us, and put us to bed. She saw to it that we had clean clothes to wear and clean sheets on our beds. Nenni took care of all Mamá's babies as they came along in quick succession. I am sure Mamá was grateful that she did not have to run up and down the stairs as often as Nenni! In a big household like Gromi's, a nanny was a necessity, and she became like a family member. Although our parents were a regular part of our lives, the daily routine was left to the nanny. Only Johanna and Martina did not come under Nenni's loving care because by the time they were born, we had a new nanny.

When Rupert was six years old, life became more serious as he and I "graduated" from the nursery to our first governess and teacher. Rupert had to start first grade. There was no elementary school nearby, so a young teacher, Fräulein Zeiner, was hired to live with us. The lessons took place in the attic of Gromi's house where Rupert and I shared a room with a balcony. Her duties were not only to teach Rupert but also to see to our daily routine the way Nenni had done. We liked our new governess a lot.

When I found out that Rupert was going to learn how to write, I asked Fräulein Zeiner if I could learn too. She gave me a copybook with double lines. She then drew the letter *i* at the beginning of each line, each one with a dot above the top of the stick. I was eager to copy them. Not knowing how important it was to write the letters exactly as they were supposed to be, I took some artistic liberty and made a little curl of smoke on the top of the stick instead of a dot. I thought that would make it look more interesting. I drew the whole page like that with all the little puffs of smoke rising in unison from my page. When I presented the first page of writing I had done, at the age of four and a half, to Fräulein Zeiner, I thought that she would be delighted, but instead she became very angry. She threw the notebook on the floor and told me in no uncertain terms that this was not what I was supposed to write. I broke out in tears and thus ended my first writing lesson.

Although my first writing lesson was a disappointment to me, I

nevertheless remember Fräulein Zeiner with gratitude. She taught me something that was immeasurably more valuable than learning to write. One day, as she was taking my siblings and me on the usual afternoon walk, I saw some little plants, flowers, moss-covered tree roots, and stones on the side of the road. I thought they were beautiful and wanted to know who made them. Fräulein Zeiner said, "God made them." "Who is God?" I asked her. She said, "God is a Spirit. We cannot see Him. He can do everything He wants to, and He knows everything. He made the trees, the flowers, the grass, and every living thing." At this young age, I was so close to the ground that I could see things that adults did not easily notice. I was elated when she told me about this God who knows everything and could do anything He wanted to do.

But then something occurred to me that made me feel sorry for Him. I had to tell her: "Fräulein, God cannot see what He has made because He is a Spirit!" Fräulein Zeiner told me that once He became a man and then He could see all that He had created.

"Where is He now?" I wanted to know. She answered, "One day, long ago, He was killed." That made me even sadder. When she saw that, she quickly added, "But now He resides in a little house in the church behind a white veil." That made me happy again. From then on, every time we went to church I looked to see this veil she was talking about. Although I could never figure out how to find "this God" behind the veil, I still believed that He lived in the church in this little house on the altar, and that was enough to give me a feeling of great reverence when I entered a church. From that time on, I had a tender love for this almighty and all-knowing God who made all living things and resides behind a white veil in the church. I never forgot this walk with Fräulein Zeiner. Even though her "theology" was not one hundred percent accurate, Fräulein Zeiner, with this simple explanation of God, instilled in my heart the love for our Creator.

One day Fräulein Zeiner told everyone that she was planning on entering a convent. She put a towel over her head to show us how she would look as a nun. Before she left, I told her to be sure to visit us, and in a typical child's manner, I asked her to bring us oranges, lemons, and sugar cubes. All of these items were very scarce. Little did I know that once she entered the convent, she would not be able to visit us or bring us gifts.

In addition to having a governess, we had a live-in piano teacher who had taught my mother and her brother Franky when they were children. When I heard that Fräulein Kupka would be giving lessons to Rupert, I asked Mamá whether I could learn to play the piano too. My enthusiasm originated from hearing Uncle Franky sit at the piano and play without looking at any music. I thought all one had to do was to sit down in front of the piano, put one's hands on the keys, and play. Then it dawned on me that one probably learned to do this by taking piano lessons. I was then only four and a half years old.

I could hardly wait to begin. The wonderful day came when I sat in front of the baby grand piano. I was sure that Fräulein Kupka would work the miracle of teaching me a waltz or some other beautiful piece of music. Instead she tried to teach me to *read* the music, letter by letter, note by note, sound by sound. Surely this might be a good way to teach children who are able to connect the letters, sounds, and symbols plus find the sounds on the keyboard, but it didn't work for me at my young age. I tried, yet I could not read the music. I was sure that I would be able to play any song I had heard, but try as I would, I could not connect the music symbols on the page with the sounds on the keyboard.

When I could not learn in this way, Fräulein Kupka became very angry and hit my fingers with a pencil and finally yelled at me that she would leave if I did not do better. I left the piano in tears, thus ending my early piano lessons. Although I can now play the piano by ear and even improvise—I play whatever I hear in my mind—I never learned to read music well.

Teachers in those days must have thought of children as little adults. Much misery could have been spared if the teachers of that generation had understood a little child psychology.

About the same time as my first writing and piano lessons, Gromi granted me a very special privilege. I was allowed to go into her "boudoir"—but only when she invited me to come in. It was not really a boudoir; it was her very private office where she sat at her antique rolltop desk and where one could see all kinds of beautiful and interesting things, such as framed photographs, vases with flowers, memorabilia, and little figurines. Gromi told me, "You may look with your eyes but not with your hands." That was my first lesson in respecting other people's property.

In her boudoir, Gromi would tell me stories about her family, which I sensed were important to her but not so much to me. But I did not dare say I did not want to listen for fear of hurting her feelings. Now I am glad that she told me these stories. Although I could not even visualize at the time what she was telling me and why, these memories remained with me and have helped me to write this book.

Included in the stories that she told me were those of her parents. Count August Breuner and Countess Agathe Breuner owned a majestic house on the Singerstrasse in the city of Vienna that was known as the Breuner Palace. There the Breuners spent the winters. Thus, they were able to enjoy the arts—concerts, the theater, and the opera—and take part in whatever social events happened to be on the agenda at the imperial court in Vienna. They also entertained in the ornate rooms of their own palace. In it was an apartment where Gromi stayed when she had to go into the city to see her dentist or to go shopping.

From her childhood Gromi knew what a well-run household was. She grew up in the Castle Grafenegg,[1] a large estate in the country. Her mother and her staff managed the household; Gromi's father and his staff took care of the grounds. Gromi, therefore, had a pattern by which to set up her own household on a somewhat smaller scale. She knew how it should function and how to make things happen.

Gromi conducted her big household with wisdom and authority. She supervised her garden and enjoyed watching her grandchildren arrive and grow. She also painted landscapes of various views on the premises and the likenesses of some of the people there. She invited her neighbor, Professor Hochenegg, a prominent doctor, to give advice on her family's health and to discuss matters of politics in which she was interested. Gromi wrote long letters to her many relatives.

Gromi was never idle; her day was well planned with different activities. She gave directions daily to the cook, the maids, the butler, and the gardener. I can still hear them say, "Jawohl, Frau Gräfin" (Very well, Countess). Although she had married a commoner and could have called herself simply "Mrs. Whitehead," she kept the title of countess from her maiden name, perhaps for the sake of authority after the death of her husband. Gromi had a quietly firm way with her staff. She was never flustered, nor did she raise her voice. I never witnessed any last-minute rush or excitement. She seemed to be able to take care of everything in good time.

Around her neck Gromi wore a watch on a long chain. It had a lid, which could be opened by pressing a little knob on the side. It was a golden watch with engravings on the lid. When we came to say, "Good morning, Gromi," she would take out her watch and hold it out to us and say, "Blow on it." Then when we blew, the lid would spring open, and we could see the face of the watch. For a long time, we thought the lid opened because we blew on it! It was fun for her as well as for us. Rupert, our scientist, was the first one to discover the real workings of this mystery.

Gromi knew the importance of self-discipline. She exercised it herself, and she wanted to teach it to us. There was a vegetable garden behind the kitchen house, which was surrounded by a hedge of red and white currant bushes. When the currants were ripe, Gromi would send Rupert and me out with little baskets to pick them, but she impressed upon us that we should not eat any berries while we were picking. In those days, it was considered unhealthy to eat uncooked fruit. Or perhaps she thought we would eat too many!

Then she would say, "Tilli [the cook] will make *Ribisel Eis* [currant sorbet]." So we eagerly picked the berries and competed to see who could pick the most in the shortest time. It was a challenge that we were glad to meet. The reward came in the form of the most delicious sorbet made by Tilli. Smooth, sweet, and cold, with the taste of berries without the seeds, it was wonderful!

Mamá loved gardening. She and her sister Mary did a lot of it at the Erlhof where flower beds ran alongside Gromi's house. The beds had hollyhocks, larkspur, monkshood, red and white phlox, and foxglove which we were told is poisonous. The entrance to the house was adorned with a flower box filled with a rare hanging azalea known as *Goldglocken* (golden bells). Gromi was very proud of this plant and made sure that it was well taken care of. Sometimes she watered it herself. The gardener tended the garden paths, which were always flawlessly raked; not one weed showed itself. There were also flowering bushes, spruce trees, tall larches, and ash trees with red berries in the fall. Gromi and her gardener had planted everything and looked after it.

Taking advantage of such natural beauty, our governess took us on walks to explore the nearby countryside. Part of our daily routine in good weather was hiking on the dirt road along the lake and taking steeper walks up the mountain that rose behind Gromi's property. We were never unattended on these excursions.

One of our lake walks took us to the Hotel Bellevue. The hotel had a breathtaking view of the snow-capped mountains across the lake.

For us, a unique feature of the hotel was the black bellboy who lived there. A black person was a rarity in Austria, and this bellboy fascinated my sister Maria, who was about four years old. This early fascination would be a foreshadowing of her interests and work as an adult. Many years later, she spent thirty-two years as a lay missionary in Papua, New Guinea, helping the people in their struggles with modern life.

Another walk led first along the lakeside and then up the steep mountain to the home of the *Honigbauer* (honey farmer). The only flat spot was the area where the house stood. His farm had a little bit of everything: cows, maybe a horse, chickens, sheep, and goats. In addition to farming, this farmer kept bees, which pollinated his fruit trees. He had apple trees, plum trees, one or two cherry trees, and a pear tree or two. All of these fruits were either preserved in jars or dried for the winter. When we arrived at his house, the farmer's wife came out smiling and gave the "dear little children" each a slice of home-baked, dark rye bread spread with honey. What a treat that was after our steep climb! Then Fräulein Zeiner bought a jar of honey to take home.

Sometimes we went with Gromi along the lakeshore on her daily walks. There were geese swimming on the lake, near the shore. When Gromi passed by, they came out of the water and went toward her with outstretched necks, pointing their beaks and hissing at her. Gromi, who always carried a parasol, pointed it at the geese and opened and closed it quickly. That was to tell the geese, "Do not hiss at me. Let me take my walk undisturbed." They understood and went back into the water. Because of this experience, I later suggested to my father that he should use parasols instead of torpedoes to frighten away the enemy!

One of the most memorable walks around the area involved a close escape. Mamá took Rupert, then five, and me, three and a half, for a walk to the Sand Riegel, a piece of land at one end of the Zeller Lake. The area was flat and sandy with large blackberry bushes growing all over. Between the blackberry bushes, the grass was lush, which was good for grazing cattle. When we went there for a walk, we always

picked blackberries in season. Little hay barns (*Heustadel*), where the farmer stored the hay for later use, stood here and there. The *Heustadel* were built from wooden logs spaced apart like a ladder, allowing air to circulate and keep the stored hay dry. The little barn had a shingled roof and a large window. One could easily climb into the haystack through the window using the logs as a foothold.

On that particular day, the farmer had his bull grazing there. The blackberry bushes must have hidden the bull from Mamá's view; she did not know he was there. The moment he discovered someone entering his territory the bull charged. Suddenly Mamá noticed him as he raced toward us. She took the two of us under her arms, ran to the nearest *Stadel*, threw each of us through the window into the hay, and then climbed in herself. Just then the bull arrived. Of course, he could not climb up the logs into the loft. He circled the *Stadel* several times, snorting. When he saw that the intruders were not to be reached, he finally trotted off. How long we were trapped in the hay log cabin I do not know. But my guess is that the farmer had an eye on the bull, and when he saw him charge, the farmer came to our rescue and sent the bull back to his stable. Mamá then took us home without further incident.

While our walks showed us the beauties of our world, we started seeing war planes in the sky above. Near the end of the war, the planes appeared over the Zeller Lake. They were the first kind of airplanes used during the war. Although their purpose was unclear to us, Gromi was not taking any chances; we were not going to become targets. The wings of the airplanes were straight and narrow, making them appear like dragonflies high up in the sky. We could see them plainly from the ground. Indeed it was exciting to see them over the lake. Gromi understood their potential danger, however, and would order us to run behind the house and stand flat against the wall when the planes were in the area. Of course, bombs could have been dropped, and we could not have done anything to save ourselves.

In Gromi's spacious garden, along the lakeshore, we learned many things from nature's bounty. In those days there was no radio, television, movie theater, shopping mall, or even electricity. *How boring!* one might think. But, no, instead we used our imaginations to turn a row of chairs into an express train and a sofa into a hospital.

The living room in the Erlhof was a perfect spot to "play train." Gromi's wicker chairs became passenger cars, with Rupert as conductor. Maria and I were the passengers. The "conductor" gave us tickets, called out stations, and announced that the train had stopped. Then Maria and I stepped off into the "station."

On rainy days, we liked to improvise with costumes. We pretended that Rupert was the king, I was the queen, and Maria, the princess. Rupert and I wore gold paper crowns made by Tante Mary, and Maria had a big white bow in her hair. When we tired of these roles, we became father, mother, and child. Rupert had no choice; he was father! I was mother, and Maria, the child.

Sometimes all the adults came together to play games with us. There were games I liked a lot such as Find the Thimble, Cat and Mouse, and Hide-and-Seek.

Gromi had a stack of educational magazines from Munich with beautifully colored steel etchings of historical scenes and events. They included fairy tales, stories in verse, and scenes from *The Iliad* and *The Odyssey*. Papá and Tante Mary acted out the story of Odysseus and the Cyclops, with Papá narrating the exciting tale.

The winter months brought other forms of entertainment. One day when Papá came home on furlough, he put on his skis and told us to stand behind him on the skis and hold onto his legs. Down we went with him over the gentle slope behind Gromi's house. That was our first time skiing.

There were other ways to be entertained in the snow. When it was the right consistency to form snowballs, Mamá and Tante Mary built a large igloo that we could stand in. We helped them make the big snowballs, which they used to form the snow house. Another day they built a snowman with a carrot for his nose and a black top hat. We all had a lot of fun on those winter days.

Still another winter activity we enjoyed was watching the men cutting ice on the lake. When the lake was frozen over with the ice at least a foot thick, the farmer would take his team of workhorses hitched to a special wooden sled and actually drive onto the ice near the shore. Then he and his men would cut each ice block about twelve by twelve by thirty-six inches, fish the ice blocks out with huge iron hooks on long poles, and load them onto the sled. The whole operation was a fascinating spectacle for the adults and even more so for us children. We watched every move, always fearing that someone might fall into the water or the ice might break with the weight of the heavy horses and the sled. It never did.

When the load was full, they took it to Gromi's icehouse. Inside the men arranged the ice blocks in such a way as to form a flight of stairs, like shelves, where the cook could set baskets, pots, or boxes of food. The ice lasted until the next winter. Only the cook had the key to the icehouse. In the early summer, wild strawberries grew over the grassy top of the icehouse. I was the only one who knew about the berries and used to pick them as a present for Mamá.

During the long, cold winter months, Gromi supplied a special entertainment for her family and guests. She cut puzzles for them. She had a special jigsaw for making puzzles set up in the living room. She brought out an interesting picture mounted on a wooden backing, cut it into many small pieces that were not easily distinguished from one another, and laid them all into a box. Then she set up a card table. Family members and visiting guests searched out the elusive puzzle pieces and fit them into special places so the picture could slowly emerge.

Gromi was a gifted person with a well-rounded education. She was interested in everything around her. She had been tutored at home, according to the custom in aristocratic families of her time. Her talents were many and varied. She would spin wool into yarn on her spinning wheel. Gromi could also read music and play the piano well, sometimes playing duets with Mamá or Uncle Franky. Gromi created and ran a well-organized household and participated in raising us children.

Those early years spent at the Erlhof, under the watchful eyes of Mamá, Gromi, and the aunts, were indeed precious ones. We learned to live as a family, where values were important. We learned to entertain ourselves, and we heard the first sounds of music that later became so much a part of our lives.

4

Two Special Occasions

The Christmas of 1914 was the first Christmas I remember. I was not quite two years old. I stood in front of the Christmas tree, which in its full height stretched from the floor to the ceiling. The soft light of its candles brightened the room. In its glow, I stood alone. A tall, slender man came toward me. He was blond, wearing a bluish-gray uniform with a high green collar and green trim on the sleeves; it was the gala uniform of the Emperor's House Regiment.

I heard someone say, "This is Uncle Werner." I looked up at him.

He bent down and gently kissed me on my forehead. I knew immediately that he was a very kind person, but I never saw him again. Uncle Werner was killed in an offensive by the Russians against the Austrian troops in Galicia on May 2, 1915. In my memory, though, Uncle Werner is still as alive today as he was on that long ago Christmas Eve.

In Austria at that time, children learned that it was the Christ Child who came at Christmastime, bringing gifts with Him. Angels were His helpers. A room was set aside to give the Christ Child privacy, and children knew they should not disturb Him.

In the Erlhof, our nursery was on the second floor. From there a big open staircase led directly into the big living room, which was called "the Hall." A week before Christmas, the Hall was closed off

"Silent Night..."

from the staircase. We were told not to use the staircase because the Christ Child with His angels was preparing a surprise for Christmas Eve in the Hall. Everyone whispered and wondered what the angels might be doing, now that Christmas was so close.

On Christmas Eve, we children were dressed in our best clothes for the holy occasion; expectation was at its height. Then, there it was—the sound of a silver bell announcing that it was time for us to go to the Hall. Slowly, with rapidly beating hearts, we went down the wide staircase. Oh, wonder! There stood the Christmas tree in its entire splendor. The Hall was illuminated in soft candlelight, magnified a million times by the brightly colored balls of glass and a glistening veil of angel hair. We just stood, taking it all in.

As we edged closer to the tree, we detected cookies hanging on golden strings. Also there was candy wrapped in colored paper, fringed at each end and fastened to the tree with silver strings. Birds of paradise with long glass tails and other colorful ornaments were visible through the fine veil of angel hair. All of this was even more wonderful because we children believed that heaven came down to earth in the person of Jesus in order to leave us presents and share His wonders.

Beside the tree, lying in a manger, was the Baby Jesus. He was smiling and held out His arms to us. His hair was curly and light, the color of the straw He was laid on. I was glad to see that He was not lying on the straw itself but on a fine white doily with lace edging. I wished so much that the Baby Jesus in the manger was real instead of waxen, and that He could move around as real babies do.

After a few moments of admiration, the entire household, family and staff, sang together "Silent Night, Holy Night." Then each person was shown the place where his or her presents were laid out on white tablecloths, covering the furniture. Everything was a surprise. Of course, we did what all children do at Christmas; we showed our presents to our parents. They admired everything, just as if they had never seen these things before. The girls usually received dolls, for which Mamá made clothes, and doll furniture. I cannot remember many of the boys' presents, but at least one Christmas a hobby horse and a stable with animals were given to Werner.

The picture of my uncle, the Christmas tree, and me remains indelibly imprinted in my mind. I will always cherish this memory of my Uncle Werner on that wonderful Christmas Eve of 1914.

Another memorable event from my childhood took place at the Erlhof when I was five and a half years old. I met my great-grandmother, Countess Agathe Breuner, for the first and only time. The occasion? It was her eighty-fifth birthday, and a celebration was arranged for her at the Erlhof. I remember seeing a photograph, taken earlier, which showed the four generations with the name of Agathe. It pleased my grandmother that her mother lived long enough to have this picture taken. I was the baby in the photo. When Great-grandmother came to visit at the Erlhof, she was accompanied by friends and relatives because Great-grandfather had died many years before. At my great-grandmother's birthday celebration, I

remember my mother's cousin, Tante Lorlein Auersperg, and one of
Papá's officers and friends, Erwin Wallner, who later married Tante
Lorlein. Erwin Wallner had a beautiful baritone voice and loved to
sing arias, and he would do so at the drop of a hat.

I remember my great-grandmother as a very old lady in black, a
little stooped over, and with many wrinkles in her face. She wore a
white round lace cap on her head with a black ribbon woven along the
edge of it. I have no recollection of her personality, but she must have
been greatly loved by her family to receive such a grand birthday
celebration.

Weeks before she came, Mamá, Tante Mary, and Tante Connie
sewed costumes for us and themselves to create tableaus as part of the
festivities after lunch. The performance was set up in the barrack on
the old tennis court. There was a little stage on which was placed an
enormous wooden picture frame. In it we were positioned like
statues, dressed in old-fashioned costumes. The grown-ups staged a
tableau of a pirate ship with its crew. Maria and I were costumed in
empire dresses, which were long with high waists and had pink
sashes. We also wore matching bonnets made of white chiffon with a
pattern of little pink roses. Rupert wore a blue-and-white-striped suit
in the same style with a black mortarboard hat. I had a second
costume that was my favorite. I was dressed as a medieval page in
dark red velvet knickers and a matching tunic edged with fur that had
a belt with a knife on the side. I wore little red velvet slippers edged
with fur and a red velvet beret also edged with fur with a red feather
stuck sideways into its band.

Gromi had a stack of old-fashioned magazines, *Münchner Bilder
Bogen*, which were actually artistic picture books for grown-ups with
gorgeous illustrations of historical events. There were also fashion
pictures from different centuries with pages of costumes from
different regions and countries of Europe. This hardcover magazine,
edited in Germany, was probably the inspiration for our tableaus.

Before the big performance, I saw the whole party walking from
the main house to the barrack, where the stage and seats were set up.
Werner, who was almost three years old, ran ahead of the party,

singing clearly with a booming voice, "Ich hatt' einen Kameraden" (I had a comrade), a song that was sung by the Austrian population and soldiers throughout the war. Fräulein Zimmermann, our governess at the time, composed a long poem and made me memorize it. I did memorize it but only by sound. I had no idea what I was saying. Fräulein had instructed me to stand up at the festive dinner table, ring my glass with my dessert spoon, and recite the poem. But, oh, after a few sentences, I had forgotten what came next, and I got stuck! There was dead silence. Embarrassment gripped me, as it did the whole dinner table. No one said a word; no one helped me, and I burst into tears. From then on and even well into adulthood, I remained tongue-tied in front of strangers. Fortunately I eventually conquered this affliction.

The next morning, a home Mass was arranged for all the guests. Because of a space problem, the Mass was held in the barrack where we had staged the still life performances. The priest had come from Zell am See and, during Mass, distributed Holy Communion. I did not know what Mass was all about and thought he was giving out peppermint candy! Since everyone went forward to get this "candy," so did I. But before I could reach the priest, someone caught me, and I was told I could not have it. Later my mother explained to me that I would have to wait until I was older to receive what they received, and she said that it was *not* peppermint candy.

Two years later, on November 20, 1920, Great-grandmother died in Goldegg bei St. Pölten, in the home of her daughter Lori. Gromi went to the funeral.

Fräulein Zimmermann told me that I must write a sympathy letter to my grandmother. I had never written a letter in my seven and a half years of life. I was stuck with a problem. Somehow I connected dying with going to heaven. Why was my grandmother sad when her mother went to heaven? Why should I write to tell my grandmother that I was sorry that her mother had died? She went to heaven. My grandmother must know that. Why should I write to her about something that she knows? What can I tell her that she does not know already? She is the grandmother who is so much older and wiser than

I am.

I do not remember what I finally wrote or whether the governess dictated something to me. But I remember distinctly thinking these thoughts and the conflict that arose from the command that I should write this letter. I am sure my great-grandmother would have helped me and consoled me in my distress if she could have. But she was in heaven. I did not understand grief that can override the understanding of things.

Although it may seem unusual for a young child to have such vivid recollections, the images of both that very special Christmas and my great-grandmother's visit will always remain with me.

5

The Postwar Era

O n November 11, 1918, the war was over. Our soldiers came back from the front in troop trains, which were overcrowded. Some were so eager to get home that they climbed onto the roofs of the railroad cars. But they did not make it home because they were swept off the trains or were beheaded by the entrances to the tunnels, which took the trains through the mountains.

The Austro-Hungarian Empire was in shambles. Hungary separated itself from Austria, as did Czechoslovakia and Croatia. Istria and South Tyrol were given to Italy by the Treaty of Versailles. Emperor Karl I of Austria went into exile with his family in 1919. The pinch of hard times was felt by all as food, textiles, and other commodities became scarce.

The borders between the Austrian provinces were closed. Anyone traveling from one province to the other was subjected to a body search if suspected by the train personnel of smuggling food. All necessities of life were difficult to obtain. Because of this on Sundays and holy days, in spite of all restrictions, droves of people went from the cities into the country to visit their "relatives" on farms in order to get vegetables, fruits, butter, and meat. If people were caught hamstering (black-marketing), the food would be confiscated, or high duties would be imposed on the items. The economy was so deflated that the government printed emergency money, which was worth nothing.

Austria was impoverished to the bone. Poor people were given a patch of land (*Schräbergarten*) on the peripheries of the cities where they could grow their own vegetables and fruits. Each patch of land contained a homemade shack for tools and was surrounded by a wire fence.

In those first days after the war, people ate dogs, cats, rabbits, and squirrels. They caught ducks and geese from other people's ponds. They ate anything just to keep alive. The bread was made of a dark crust stuffed with cornmeal that was mixed with sawdust. Materials for clothing were mixed with paper. String was made of paper, twisted tightly, but of course it dissolved when it got wet.

Although we had a very good cook, she could not prepare the meat. No matter what she did, it was as tough as shoe leather—especially the boiled beef. After the adults had finished the meal, we children would sit for hours and hours, chewing and chewing the unchewable meat. In those days, children had to eat what was put on their plates, whether they liked it or not, and could not leave the table until their plates were cleared. The adults seemed to be able to chew the meat, but we could not. Spending hours into the afternoon, my sister Maria suffered greatly, battling with this tough meat.

The pork was even worse. One could say, "Well, it is better to have tough meat than none." But that did not solve the problem of chewing it! The pork was not only tough but also unappetizing. It took all my willpower to put a bite of pork shoulder into my mouth. I sat after lunch—which is the main meal in Austria served at 1:00 p.m.—and chewed and chewed and chewed. When Mamá's maid saw me still eating alone in the dining room around three o'clock one afternoon, she asked me what was the matter. I said I could not chew the meat. She asked me, "Would you let me eat this piece of meat?" referring to the meat that I had already chewed and placed back on the plate. I said, "Yes, if you want it." She took it and ate it, finishing all the meat on my plate, thus allowing me to leave the table. I embraced her for this unselfish deed.

Sauerkraut was another dish that was not easy to swallow because of the very strong smell. The odor was due to the method of preparation. Onion sauce accompanied every meat dish, supposedly to enhance it. Unfortunately some of us did not like the onion sauce. Another very healthy, but hated, vegetable was the red beet. Beets came from Gromi's vegetable garden. We did not like them, although we were told that they contained iron, which was needed for a healthy body. There were also the yellow beets (*die Rucken*), which were raised primarily to feed the pigs. But what do you do if there is a food shortage of other, more appetizing foods? You eat *die Rucken*. In those days, Werner prayed, "Lieber Gott lass Mehlspeis wachsen!" (Dear God, please let desserts grow!).

Sugar and flour were Papá's presents to the family. In Hungary the sugar was made from sugar beets. Since Papá's route home from the navy took him through Hungary, he was able to buy some sugar to bring back to Austria, where it was a thing of the past. He gave some to Gromi and the rest to us. He also brought some flour—*real*, white flour that was not mixed with sawdust. Pure, white flour was a precious commodity in Austria and unavailable for a long time. Mamá put it into a wooden bin for storage, to be used slowly as the need arose. To her dismay, she discovered only a few days later that mice had gnawed a hole in one corner of the bin and had helped themselves to the flour, leaving their droppings mixed in. What to do? Since the flour was so precious, Mamá and the cook sieved the droppings out of the flour. I remember watching the procedure, and it took some time to accomplish the task. Mamá then put the cleaned flour into tin boxes.

One morning I heard Mamá say that she must take Werner to Vienna because he had "bow legs." As a result of the poor nourishment during the war years, his legs needed to be straightened by a specialist. Of course, I wanted to go to Vienna too. I must have heard stories from Gromi about how beautiful and exciting Vienna was. Mamá told me I could not come along because there was nothing wrong with my legs. "But," she said, "if you are good and don't cry and will wait until you are older, *you* will travel to Vienna and to many other places." With that promise, I resolved to wait until my time for traveling came. Mamá had no idea that she had made a prediction that *did* come true many years later.

The soldiers who came back from the war did not find a homeland that took care of their needs, a homeland where peace and security would soon help them recover from what they had suffered in body and soul. Instead, they came back to a boiling pot of social changes. There were no jobs, no food, no clothing. Many soldiers who had fought bravely for their country were walking from door to door, sometimes in rags, on crutches, begging for food. The soldiers and sailors who went from door to door were also looking for a little work so they could buy cigarettes and anything they needed, perhaps a railroad ticket to visit their relatives. I remember one Italian navy man who came to our door and asked my father whether he could work for him. He advertised himself in Italian as "forte come un toro" (strong like a bull). My father was intrigued by his ingenuity and hired him to do garden work. He had dark curly hair and spoke only Italian. We called him "Toro." He stayed a while and then went on.

After the end of the war, the Austrian Navy ceased to exist, and Yugoslavia and Italy took over its ships. Some of our naval officers who were Italians or Yugoslavs were willing to serve under the new regimes. But for Papá, that was impossible. His loyalty was to Austria, victorious or defeated. Before he came home, we were told that the war was over. Papá was coming home for good, but he was very sad, and we were told to be very kind to him. Only later did I realize what an adjustment my father had to make from his life as the captain of a submarine to the position of the head of a family with five young children. When Papá returned to the Erlhof, he wanted to find a home for us as soon as possible because we had been living in Gromi's house.

To show his appreciation to Gromi, Papá decided that before we left the Erlhof, he would do something special for her. Up to the end of World War I, the lighting in the Erlhof consisted of kerosene lamps with large white lampshades. At that time an electric power station was being built high up in the mountains near Zell am See, so Papá and Uncle Franky worked to wire the Erlhof for the blessing of electric lights. Gromi was delighted at the prospect of illuminating the living room and other rooms with the flick of a switch. Everyone was looking forward to this momentous event.

We assembled in the living room to watch the first bulb light up, but when the electricity was switched on, we could see only a thin rose-colored wire inside the bulb. Too many people had turned on their switches at the same time, and the powerhouse did not have enough power. So the kerosene lamps were in use again for a while until enough power became available. Papá and Uncle Franky could put the wiring in—but not the electricity.

After the electric wiring was installed, it was time to move out of Gromi's house. Papá did not want to impose any longer on Gromi's generosity. Papá and Mamá looked around various parts of Austria to find a house that was adequate for a big family. But they could not find anything suitable. Mamá's brother Franky owned the house next to Gromi's property, which had previously been a hotel. He offered it to my parents until they could find something to buy.

It was right on the lakeshore and just big enough for our family, the cook, two maids, the governess (for the two older children, Rupert and me), and the nanny (for the three little ones: Maria, Werner, and Hedwig). The house was called "Hotel Kitzsteinhorn," after the high mountain across the lake. The Kitzsteinhorn was built before the war, close to the water's edge. At that time, a pier reached

Hotel Kitzsteinhorn

From memory – A v.T

out into the lake to accommodate the motorboat from Zell am See, which stopped there for the convenience of hotel guests. During the war, however, the hotel became vacant, and the pier fell into disrepair, after which Uncle Franky bought the property.

At that time, girls did not go out to make a life for themselves before they married. Therefore, Mamá's two unmarried sisters lived with Gromi. Despite the fact that Gromi had two single daughters in her house, she did not want us to leave her. She had already endured loss. Her oldest son, John, a test pilot in England's Royal Air Force, was killed in a test flight of one of the first planes to be used in warfare. Her second son, Franky, eventually worked in the travel bureau in Zell am See. Her third son, Robert, lived in Hungary.

The Erlhof was built for her children. Without them, it meant nothing to Gromi. Now her beloved daughter Agathe was going to depart with her husband and their five children, three of them born in the Erlhof. She could not bear the thought of parting with them, but it had to be done. The change was made so that we hardly noticed it. One day we had a new home half a mile down the road from Gromi's Erlhof.

There was also a new baby on the way, and when it was the right time, Mamá went back to the Erlhof. Johanna was born in the very same room where three other young von Trapps had found their way into the world. I remember the first time I saw her. She was lying in a baby basinette with a canopy of delicate curtains that had little flowers printed on them. The nurse moved the curtains away, and there was the new baby with big brown eyes.

Hedwig, two years old, took a look at her baby sister and said, "Ich werd mit der Lute kommen! [I will come with the switch!]" (unable to pronounce *Rute*, Hedwig called the switch *Lute*). Then Johanna started to cry. Hedwig must have heard this phrase addressed to her many times from her nanny and so thought this was what one said to little children! But Johanna obviously did not like the sound of it. Someone took Hedwig out of the room.

After a few weeks in the Erlhof with Gromi, Mamá returned to the Kitzsteinhorn. While our family lived there, Rupert once came down the many steps that led to the place where the pier should have been a bit too fast. He fell head over heels into the water. Perhaps that accident triggered the repair of the pier.

One day some men appeared who were appointed to do the job. In order to build the new pier, the men had to drive heavy wooden posts into the bottom of the lake. While standing on a scaffold, they placed a huge iron block with six handles on top of the post, to be used as a hammer. As they began to work, they started to sing a song, not to the post, not to each other, not because it was a beautiful, sunny day and they felt like singing, but to coordinate their blows on the post. The rhythm of the song told each man when to lift the block and when to let it fall. It was a very wonderful sight to see the men at work.

As we watched them, we also learned their song, never to forget it. The words are in the local dialect of the Pinzgau. The song went like this:

Auf und z'am	Up and down
Der Tag is lang	The day is long
Der Schaegl is schwar	The sledge hammer is heavy
Von Eis'n er war	It is made of iron
Da Lercha Kern	The larch post
Er geht nit gern	Does not want to move
Er muass hinein	It must go down
Durch Sand und Stein	Through sand and stone
Durch Stein und Sand	Through stone and sand
In's Unterland	Into the land below
HOCH AUF!	LIFT UP!

The melody to this song was not written down. If it had been written down, it would have become a hit song in the United States! But it was forever imprinted into the memories of the men who sang it probably thousands of times, and into our memories as we watched them pound the posts into the "land below." The rhythm of this song gave them the coordination to do the otherwise impossible. HOCH AUF!

The motorboat was no longer in operation, and we did not own a boat. So Papá bought a horse and buggy with a few warm blankets to keep us warm as we traveled around the lake to the town on errands. The horse was lodged under the balcony of our house where Papá had built a stable. For us it was a great thing to have a horse and buggy for our own use, even though we children did not ride in it very often. The horse's name was Dagie, after a friend of Papá's from the navy, whose name was Dagobert Müller. Papá took care of the horse himself.

To improve our diet, and to provide entertainment, Papá bought chickens—nine hens and a rooster. When he saw how much we loved the chickens and enjoyed finding the eggs, he bought three dwarf chickens just for us—a rooster and two hens. The dwarf hens laid little eggs, and we were delighted.

Every day we went to watch and feed them. Papá kept the chickens in a little wooden building next to our "hotel," and he made small boxes where they could lay their eggs. Every morning he collected the eggs. One morning, however, there were only two hens and the eggs were crushed. What had happened? There were feathers on the floor and little pools of blood on the ground, even outside. Who had taken the chickens? How had he gotten into the chicken house, whoever he was?

Papá went all around the chicken house to find some tracks on the ground in order to find out who the robber was. That afternoon he took us on a walk onto the wooded hillside behind the house to look for mushrooms. As we came down the hill, he saw one of our chickens half buried under the fallen leaves. Then we saw another and yet another. Who was this mysterious thief that left part of the spoil?

Perhaps it was an animal. A person would surely have taken them all.

So Papá constructed a big wooden trap. He covered the far end of the trap with a piece of chicken wire. The trap was constructed so that when an animal went in and got to the end of the trap, the door would fall down behind him. Papá set this trap into the entrance of the chicken house.

The next two days were quiet. Nothing happened. But on the third day the thief was caught. It was a huge, gray wild cat. I had never seen a wild cat before; therefore, I was fascinated.

One day there was excitement in Zell am See to rival our chicken thief. A moving picture film came to town and was to be shown! That was a very novel event in 1919. The film was advertised as a picture where animals and people could move, just as in real life. Impossible! But the promoters claimed it was true.

How I wanted to see that film! But only Rupert, then eight years old, was allowed to go. I stayed home, being told I was "too young." I questioned Rupert about the film when he came back home, and he confirmed that the pictures really moved. I would not see my first movie until several years later in Vienna.

In the Kitzsteinhorn, our schoolroom was in the attic. From a point where the roof sloped, a curtain was suspended to hide the family's trunks and suitcases stored there. We called this area the "North Pole." When Stutz von Jedina visited, we played all kinds of wild games there, most of them imported by Stutz! War games, Red Indian, and Cops and Robbers—all of the games were accompanied by wild gestures and fierce words, but we never hit or hurt each other. Sometimes we hid in houses, which we formed with our schoolroom furniture; other times we were prisoners bound by imaginary rope. Our imaginations ran wild, and when we were tired, we smoked a make-believe peace pipe.

When the dinner bell rang, we knew it was time to clean up. No more imaginary surprise attacks from the dark, awesome place behind the curtains where the trunks stood! We put the furniture in order, washed our hands, and went down to the living room to wait for the meal. The days when Stutz came to see us were the highlights of our time at the Kitzsteinhorn. His visits were a pleasant diversion from our daily routine. I adored Stutz.

It was 1919 when we settled in to live at the Kitzsteinhorn. Our dear Nenni had left, and in her stead the "little ones," baby Johanna included, came under the care of a new nanny. We older ones called her "the Dragoner."[1] Of course, we addressed her as "Fräulein" (Miss). She was rather stern, with her sparse black hair pulled straight back into a little knot on the back of her head. The Dragoner always wore a white nurse's uniform and spoke with a deep voice, using the mannerisms of a sergeant.

The Dragoner loved baby Johanna and disliked Hedwig. She often punished Hedwig by taking away her favorite doll, Liesl. The nanny used to make Maria, Hedwig, and Werner, who resisted her at times, sit quietly on a bench while baby Johanna slept. Then when Johanna awoke, they had to take their naps. My sister Maria is still puzzled by this arrangement, but a story that she recently told me may shed some light on this extraordinary ruling.

At one time, the Dragoner most likely went to check on Johanna sleeping in her crib and left Maria, Werner, and Hedwig for a moment in the adjacent playroom. Suddenly she heard a loud bump and a child screaming. Rushing into the next room, she found a crying Hedwig on the floor in her overturned high chair. Werner, trying to prove his strength, had pushed the high chair over. The nurse picked up Hedwig, who was frightened but unhurt. After a stern reprimand, she told Werner that he would have to go to Mamá for a spanking.

Meanwhile, Maria, who had overheard the punishment pronounced, ran quickly for her doll's pillow, inserting it into the back of Werner's pants to soften the blow, at the same time that the Dragoner was trying to soothe the sobbing child. Werner, fortified for the paddling, was escorted to Mamá's room by the nanny, who left him there. Mamá, who never spanked us anyway, inquired about the mishap and, upon finding the pillow, was touched by Maria's compassion. Then Mamá spoke kindly to Werner and kept him with her for a while before sending him back to the Dragoner.

Why did Mamá hire such a person to take care of her little ones?

The only explanation I can think of is that there was no one else available at that time when a nanny was sorely needed.

The older ones, Rupert and I, did not fare much better. Since there was no school on our side of the lake, it was necessary for us to be tutored at home. Fräulein Zimmermann, from northern Germany, became our governess. It quickly became evident to me that Fräulein disliked Rupert and loved me. She should never have become a teacher; she simply did not understand children. She constantly had a switch ready for Rupert, although I did not see any good reason for that kind of threat. She assigned me, his younger sister, to watch over him so he would not do anything that was forbidden. This responsibility did not help our relationship. All I remember as a response from Rupert for my efforts to keep him on the "right path" was, "That is none of your business."

In addition to the switch, Fräulein was always ready with sarcastic remarks directed at Rupert and made fun of him at every opportunity. What a terrible experience for a child! We never told our parents about her treatment of him. We considered Fräulein to be without blame because she was an adult and in charge of us.

Fräulein tried to teach me mathematics. I especially remember division. Because I was only six, I did not understand what she explained to me. When I was not able to master division, she called me lazy. I do not know whether Rupert could learn from her either, but I suspect not.

I recall sitting in an unfamiliar room, in front of a lady I did not know, and being asked questions I could not answer. I believe I was in a classroom and being given a test at the end of first grade. Needless to say, I failed. From that time on, I did not have any more lessons with Fräulein Zimmermann. She departed, claiming that Tante Joan, age eighteen and still living with Gromi, needed a tutor. That was a blessing for us. Fräulein Zimmermann's best service to us was recommending the next governess, who fortunately was an excellent teacher. Her name was Fräulein Freckmann, and she was from Bremen, Germany. Well educated herself, she was determined to give us the best possible education.

During the turbulent days following the end of the war with food shortages and the lack of all daily necessities, a levelheaded person like Fräulein Freckmann was a blessing. Throughout Austria, everyone was affected by the aftermath of the war; the change from monarchy to a makeshift government created insecurity and confusion. Even traveling became extremely difficult. My parents were looking for a permanent home to buy, but they could not find anything suitable for our big family. Another temporary solution, however, was already on the horizon.

6

Years of Change

~ ❦ ~

We stayed about a year and a half in the Hotel Kitzsteinhorn. Life continued as usual with lessons, walks, and our daily routine. During the summer of 1920, the glaciers melted, and the lake rose so high that the water flooded into the kitchen almost to the top of our stove. All the food that was stored in the kitchen had to be brought upstairs, and the mice started getting into everything that was edible. Gromi again opened the dining room of the Erlhof to us, and we took our meals there since it was just a short distance away. We had to pass by a meadow where a bull was grazing; therefore, Fräulein made sure that we did not wear bright red clothing on our way to Gromi's.

It must have been a difficult time for Papá and Mamá. Johanna was a baby, and the family of six children needed a place to live since the whole downstairs of the Kitzsteinhorn was waterlogged. Mamá's youngest brother, Bobby Whitehead, offered a place he owned in Klosterneuburg, close to the Danube and about a half hour's train ride from Vienna.

Uncle Bobby's property, called the "Martinschlössl" (Martin's little castle), was a former summer residence of Maria Theresa (1717–80), empress of Austria. The place was in excellent condition, with a caretaker's house, a greenhouse, an orchard, and a garden. In the middle of the courtyard, between the main house and the annex, was a round garden bed of roses.

It was a perfect place for our big family because the food shortage continued, and we could grow our own fruits and vegetables, raise chickens, and keep a cow and also a pig to eat the garbage. Papá's orderly, Franz Stiegler, and his wife, Marie, were of peasant stock, and they were willing to take care of the barnyard. They had been caretakers of our house in Pola during the war, so we knew them well. Uncle Bobby's house was going to be our home until Papá and Mamá could find a suitable one for us. Little did they know that Mamá would not live to see her family in a place of their own.

The Martinschlössl was unfurnished, so our parents decided to reclaim all the furniture they had left in Pola. Doing that was not an easy undertaking, however. Papá could not set foot into Pola, which was now Italian territory. As the commander of an Austrian submarine, he was blacklisted and would have been arrested if he had appeared in Italy. So it was decided that Mamá would make the trip to Pola to fetch our furniture.

I remember the November day when Mamá put on her black gloves and arranged her hat with the black net veil covering her face. She kissed us all good-bye and reminded us to be good while she was away. Mamá took her lady's maid, Peppina, with her. In Pola, the Stieglers assisted in the big job of crating furniture and belongings to be sent by freight to Klosterneuburg. The whole process took six weeks.

Papá went from our temporary home, the Kitzsteinhorn, to Klosterneuburg, to be there to help Mamá when the furniture arrived. We children were invited to the home of Mamá's cousin for the Christmas holidays. Under the protection and able guidance of Fräulein Freckmann, our governess, with a nanny and a maid, all six of us children embarked on the train headed for the station of St. Pölten.

My only recollection of this trip is a border incident related to hamstering. We traveled second class, which meant that we had a compartment for ourselves that consisted of two long benches facing each other, where four grown-ups could easily sit in a row. The seats were upholstered in blue or green. Overhead were shelves made of iron bars and netting for the luggage. We needed two compartments to accommodate all of us comfortably. The nanny and Johanna, the baby, were in the second compartment.

At one of the stations along the way a lady, dressed in black with a hat and veil, boarded the train. She asked if she could sit with us in our compartment. Fräulein must have given her permission. The woman proceeded to tell us a story about her dying grandmother.

At the border the guards came in to check the luggage for duty purposes. They saw the lady and asked whether she was one of our group. She told the guards the story of the dying grandmother. Becoming suspicious, an official told her to get up. She started to cry. Then the guards searched her baggage and told her to come with them. Later somebody said she was smuggling butter and had it tied in little packages around her waist like a belt. The guards found it when they searched her. Needless to say, she did not return to sit with us.

Arriving at the station in St. Pölten, we were met by a coachman driving an open carriage drawn by two horses. There were two long benches on either side. The ride over a stony dirt road seemed to take an eternity to me. I was tired from the long train trip, but the ride in the shaking carriage, the fresh air, and the new surroundings revived me as the trip went on.

Our destination was the Goldegg Castle, where Mamá's cousin, Adolph Auersperg, lived with his wife, Gabrielle, and their seven children, who were almost the same ages as we were. The oldest one, Karl Adolph, was only one year younger than Rupert was. We immediately felt at home in the beautiful castle. Tante Gabrielle welcomed us with open arms, kisses, and smiles. She personally showed us to the rooms that had been set aside for us, then showed us the way down the big, wide staircase, over the long black-and-white checkered marble floors of the corridor, to the dining room where we would have supper with the family.

All was new and different. There was so much space, much more than where we had lived previously. There were such long corridors with high ceilings. But as children do, we got used to our new surroundings in a few days.

I remember that Christmas of 1920 very clearly. To my astonishment, the children were allowed to help decorate the Christmas tree. We made chains from different colored paper strips, wrapped candies in tissue paper, and fringed them on each end with scissors. This was very new to us because in Gromi's home, we had to wait until the bell rang on Christmas Eve before we were allowed to enter the decorated Hall.

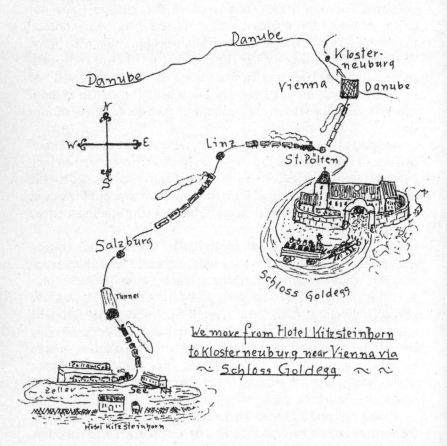

We move from Hotel Kitzsteinhorn to Klosterneuburg near Vienna via ~ Schloss Goldegg ~ ~ ~

In the Castle Goldegg, we sang "Silent Night," as we had done at
the Erlhof. There were presents for us, but the atmosphere was not
quite as awe inspiring as it had been in Gromi's house. Perhaps we
had grown up a bit. In addition, actually participating in the
preparations had taken away from the element of surprise.

While we spent Christmas of 1920 in the beautiful castle with our
relatives, Papá and Mamá made the Martinschlössl ready for our
arrival. Shortly after Christmas, on Friday, January 13, 1921, we said
good-bye to our lovely and gracious relatives and the Goldegg Castle.
Again the carriage with two horses and the driver took us to the train
heading for Klosterneuburg. After a twenty-minute uphill walk from
the station we arrived at the Martinschlössl, on the Martinstrasse,
and were happily reunited with our parents in our new home.

The house was elegant, and our furniture that had come from Pola
was just as beautiful as what we had seen in Gromi's house and the
Hall at the Erlhof. We had lived so long in places in which nothing

belonged to us that it took time to believe these things were really ours. We soon grew used to coming and going through the green front door with its shiny brass handles and door knocker.

Rupert, Maria, and I were assigned to the top floor. Also on this floor were two rooms for the maids and one for our cook. A small winding staircase led down to the next floor and could be closed off at the bottom by a door. On the second floor were the dining room, the living room, our parents' bedroom, and oh!—what luxury—a bathroom with a tub! Across from the dining room were the nursery and the children's playroom. A big staircase led down to the street level. Papá's library was there, as were a dining room for the domestic help, and a pantry and a kitchen with an exit into the spacious yard.

Shortly after we settled in, we had a surprise. In the middle of the night Fräulein Freckmann was sent to Vienna to fetch a midwife for Mamá. We had no telephone, so Fräulein Freckmann had to walk to the train station, take the local train, pick up the midwife, and repeat the whole process in reverse. She was gone at least four hours. We knew only that she was going to Vienna and would be back in the morning. In those days, we children were not made aware when a new baby was on the way. Mamá's clothing, being full to begin with, was very concealing.

The next morning, February 17, 1921, we were introduced to our newest baby sister. She had big dark eyes and a very round head like all our babies had. We were delighted! What shall we call her? Mamá and Papá had run out of ideas. Mamá teased us: "Perhaps we should call her *Dillenkräutl* [little dill plant]." No! For days we thought and thought of a good name for our new baby sister.

Finally someone suggested the name Martina. Of course! That was it! Martina fit perfectly because of the Martinschlössl, the Martinstrasse, where the house stood, and the Martinskirche (the church of St. Martin) close by. We all agreed the new baby was to be called "Martina."

Now Papá and Mamá's family was complete—Rupert, Agathe, Maria, Werner, Hedwig, Johanna, and Martina. Life had resumed its familiar patterns, this time in our new home. We older children were still tutored by Fräulein Freckmann. She structured our days so that we knew exactly what to do and when: lessons in the morning, lunch, playtime, a midafternoon walk, and *jause* at four o'clock. *Jause* was an Austrian version of afternoon tea; we enjoyed milk and bread with butter and jam. After that interlude, Fräulein set us to do our homework. Dinner was at seven-thirty, and then we went to bed.

Fräulein gave each of us individual instruction according to what grade we were in. She welcomed our questions and gave us satisfying answers. We studied the usual elementary school curriculum with arts and crafts and singing added. We sang from a beautifully illustrated book, a gift from Gromi, called *Sang und Klang Fuer's Kinderherz* (*Songs and Sounds for the Child's Heart*).

In addition to the songs we learned with Fräulein Freckmann, there was a gramophone in the playroom. We had all kinds of records, including some wonderful concert music. We listened to the famous tenor Caruso, singing his arias from *I Pagliacci* and *Figaro*. We clapped our hands and marched along with the rhythm of two well-known Austrian marches. I still remember the "Blue Danube Waltz" by Johann Strauss and Mozart's "Eine Kleine Nachtmusik." Rupert and I listened to these records for hours on rainy days. Liszt's "Hungarian Rhapsody" and Beethoven's "Violin Concerto in D" were two of my favorites.

One day Fräulein Freckmann took Rupert and me on an outing to Vienna to see one of the first films, *The Miracle of the Snow Shoe*. It was a ski film and my first time to see a movie. I loved the beautiful pictures of winter scenes. It was ironic that this movie was shown in the Urania, a building where we would give a concert many years later.

To me, Fräulein Freckmann's most important contribution to our education was the religious training she gave us. She taught us the Old and New Testaments using a children's version. Most of Austria was Catholic, so she used a catechism to explain the Ten Commandments and rules of the Catholic Church and their application to daily life. Most important was attending Holy Mass on Sunday. Neglecting this was a "mortal sin." We learned that in case anyone, even our parents, wanted us to commit a sin, we should refuse to obey. According to these teachings, we were determined never to miss Mass on Sundays.

This caused us a dilemma. Papá was Protestant, since the German von Trapps were Lutherans. We did not know this. What could we do when one Sunday morning Papá wanted to take us all on a picnic in the woodlands along the banks of the Danube? My sister Maria told Papá that we had to go to Mass. We went to church with Fräulein Freckmann, came home, put away our coats and prayer books, and went into our playroom. Suddenly—in came Papá. He was very upset and appeared to be offended by something we had done. Papá was always calm and kind; we had never seen him otherwise. He felt that his paternal right had been violated by his own children and Fräulein Freckmann, and he let us know it in no uncertain terms. We were stunned!

About half an hour later, Papá returned to us like a summer breeze. He said that he was sorry, that he hadn't understood. He said, "Now let's go on that picnic." We had a wonderful outing with roasted apples on a stick and potatoes baked in hot ashes.

That was the only time that a conflict between religious teachings and parental authority had an effect upon our family. Papá never once interfered with our religious duties after that incident. Later on, it was suggested to him that he join the Catholic Church for the sake of his children. He had some serious conversations with a Capuchin priest and decided to take the step. From then on, he went with us to Mass, and all was well.

On Saturday evenings, unbeknownst to our parents, Fräulein Freckmann attended Bible study and lessons on early Christian liturgy in another part of town. While she was away we were supposed to entertain ourselves quietly. One winter evening, we discovered a new form of entertainment. There was a coal-burning stove made of iron in our playroom, and when the coals got hot, they had to be shaken down with an iron poker before new coals were put on top. Werner had the great idea of leaving the poker in the red-hot coals until it also turned red. Then he and I took turns burning designs into the floor in front of the stove.

Our designs turned out beautifully and also created a wonderful aroma of burnt wood. It didn't occur to us that our activity could be dangerous. The stove was far away from anything that could burn, but we ruined the floor! We had such a good time that Fräulein Freckmann's wrath was totally unexpected. When she saw our designs, she was too enraged to do anything except send us to bed. Then she disappeared into her room. We got together the next morning and wrote letters of apology. They seemed to pacify her, and since the house hadn't burned down and our parents never learned about it, everything returned to normal with Fräulein Freckmann.

The Martinschlössl was an estate with a beautifully designed set of buildings with orchards that sloped to the train tracks. It was just the right size for our family, which consisted of Papá, Mamá, seven children, the cook, three maids, a governess, a nanny, and the Stiegler family, Franz and Marie, with three of their children. There was plenty of room for everyone, and we could wander around on the grounds wherever we wanted, with one restriction. When we arrived at the Martinschlössl, we children were told that we should not pick the fruit in the orchard since it all belonged to our uncle. Because Uncle Bobby came to visit from time to time and never talked to us about his "forbidden" fruit, I think the restriction was probably invented to prevent us from eating unripe fruit.

A household in those days did not have the conveniences we have today; therefore, many hands were needed to do the work. In the annex of this new home, we had three cows, chickens, one or two pigs. There was also a vegetable garden. Papá had a lot to do to oversee the barnyard and thus conferred with Franz daily.

Mamá oversaw the household in a quiet, efficient way. I never saw her angry, flustered, or impatient. The maids and the cook who had come with us from Zell am See adored her, as did all of the staff. At the Martinschlössl, a young nanny, Elfride, was put in charge of our little ones. She had a hard time with our three lively youngest von Trapps, all under the age of five, but she was able to teach them many songs to keep them happy. In order to use up some of their excess energy,

Elfride took them on long walks.

One day Mamá called us all together and said, "I invited Tante Connie and Connie Baby to come and live with us. In Ireland there is a terrible war, and they are not safe. You must accept Connie Baby as one of your sisters because she has lost her father and has no brothers and sisters." We promised to do just that. Of course, we older children already knew them from our time together at the Erlhof during World War I, after which Tante Connie and Connie Baby had returned to Ireland.

The civil war in Ireland solved our nursery problem. It was natural to put Tante Connie in charge of the little ones. Tante Connie loved children, she had a good heart and a sense of humor, and she could maintain discipline. Mamá was glad to have an intelligent relative in the house to discuss children and housekeeping. Tante Connie's philosophy of life was "live and let live." She knew what heartache was, having lost her husband, our Uncle Werner, in the war.

Christmas Day 1921 fell on a Sunday. During Mass I felt sick and told Fräulein Freckmann so. She took me home. I remember lying on a little sofa in front of the fireplace in my parents' room. The doctor said it was strep throat and recommended that I stay in bed until my fever was gone. Within a few days, Rupert, Werner, Maria, Hedwig, and Martina were sick. The nursery turned into a sick room, and the doctor diagnosed scarlet fever, which was spreading all over Klosterneuburg. Mamá and Tante Connie cared for the sick ones in the nursery, and Frau Stiegler prepared two rooms in the annex for those who recovered or were not ill. Johanna, Connie Baby, and I were placed there under Fräulein Freckmann's care.

Mamá took care of baby Martina, who was very sick with scarlet fever. Sometime in January, Mamá became ill. We were not allowed to see Mamá in her bedroom because she had such a severe case of scarlet fever. An adult case of scarlet fever was often very serious and left side effects. Mamá was taken to the Sanatorium Loew in Vienna and was there, off and on, for eight months before returning to us. It was August, and we had all recovered many weeks before. I was very happy that she was home again.

Covered with a camel's hair blanket, she was very weak and was sitting in a wheelchair. "Now I'm home for good," she said happily, "but I can't walk anymore. I'll have to learn to walk all over again." "I'll teach you to walk again," I said. She seemed pleased, even though she knew I would not be able to fulfill my promise because of my young age.

A week passed. At six o'clock on Sunday morning, September 3, 1922,[1] I awoke to the sound of the little bell ringing in the spire of the Martinskirche.

This is for Mamá, I thought, knowing that the bell rang only to announce that someone had died. I slipped back to sleep until Tante Connie came in, telling us it was time to get up.

Rupert, Maria, Werner, Hedwig, and I were taken downstairs and told that we were going to Vienna to visit Gromi. Johanna and Martina stayed behind with Tante Connie. As we got into Uncle Bobby's car, I asked if I might say good-bye to Mamá, completely forgetting about the bell I had heard earlier.

Tante Connie replied, "No, Mamá is very tired and still asleep."

Uncle Bobby delivered us to the Breuner Palace in Vienna, where Gromi had an apartment. We stayed there several days, and Papá visited us each day. We asked about Mamá: "Is she better? When can we see her?"

How hard it must have been for Papá to hear our questions without telling us that Mamá had died! After a few days, Uncle Bobby again loaded us into his car and drove us to Hungary, where he owned a house in the middle of a plum orchard. The trip with Uncle Bobby was my first in a car. In those days, the roads were muddy and filled with holes. The car was an early model, an open vehicle. Uncle Bobby, knowing that there were no places to stop for food, gas, or other necessities, drove us over the muddy roads of Austria and Hungary at a speed that defies description. He must have decided to drive nonstop to his house in Hungary! The mud sprayed in all directions as his wheels hit the potholes filled with muddy water. Every pedestrian who walked on the side of the road got a shower unless he was quick enough to jump into a field. For me, it was a hair-raising experience. Finally, after what seemed unending hours, we arrived at Uncle Bobby's house. He, a bachelor, was in a difficult situation, charged with the duty of delivering to this house his motherless nieces and nephews, who were unaware of their mother's death.

After a few days, Papá joined us. He called his children together and sat down on a little sofa in the living room. We all sat on the floor in front of him, and he told us that Mamá had gone to heaven. He did not cry, nor did he tell us a long story. He simply said that she would not be in Klosterneuburg when we returned. Some of us started to cry, and Tante Connie tried to comfort us. "Now you will be our mother," I said to her. I did not really mean for her to replace Mamá, but in my nine-year-old mind, I sensed that a mother was needed.

It may seem unusual that Mamá's children were whisked away at the time of her death. We were not allowed to be with our mother during her last hours; nor could we accompany her to her last resting place on earth. Much later Papá told us that he wanted us to remember Mamá the way we had known her—smiling, happy, and healthy. Perhaps he remembered his own sorrow when he and Uncle Werner had closed the coffin of their beloved mother, and he wanted to spare his children that grief.

In Klosterneuburg my bed was positioned near a window. When lying in bed, I could see into the dark sky. One night as I looked out I discovered one very bright star. Now that Mamá was not with us anymore, I pictured her living on this star so that she could look down and watch over us.

7

Our New Home
Near Salzburg

After Mamá was laid to rest, we came back from Hungary and returned to an empty house. Yes, the furniture was there and all in order as usual; the staff was there, and Fräulein Freckmann had come back from her vacation. The Stieglers were there. The gardener, Gustl, and his helper, Oskar, took care of the vegetable garden and orchard as usual. Tante Connie came back with us from Hungary to supervise the household for Papá. But it was still an empty house; its soul was gone, the sweet presence of Mamá, which had pervaded the household, was missing, and dust settled on the furniture. I wondered about that. Mamá once showed me how to dust: "Take away, one by one, each item that stands on the furniture—books, trinkets, a little figurine, a photo in a frame—dust it, dust under it, place it back where you took it from, and set it down the same way it was when you took it away." She must have dusted the living room and dining room herself while we were having our lessons upstairs. Nobody saw to it anymore. It was noticeable. Dust settled everywhere.

Papá looked for some work outside the house. I believe he could not endure the void that Mamá's passing had left. He had to do something to occupy his mind. He tried to find a job at the only marine establishment left to Austria, the Danube Steamship Company (*Donaudampfshiffartsgeselschaft*). But soon he quit when he found out "there was too much corruption in this company," as I remember him saying.

Uncle Bobby invited him back to Hungary for the boar and pheasant hunts. There he met his friends Karl Auersperg and Franky Whitehead, Mamá's second brother. He also visited Tante Nesti, Gromi's sister, and sought advice from her.

Every time he came back home from Hungary, we greeted him with great enthusiasm. We rushed down the big winding staircase and jumped right into his arms. He did not have enough arms for all of his seven children, but he kissed us all one by one.

After Mamá's death, Papá wanted to introduce us to the outside world. One evening Papá and Tante Connie took the four oldest children, Rupert, Maria, Werner, and me, to Vienna to see the opera *Hansel and Gretel*. At one point in the opera, the stepmother put a pan of eggs on the stove and stepped aside to sing her aria. To Werner, age six, who was watching the stove in rapt attention, the aria seemed too long. Standing up at his seat in our box, he shouted down to the stage, "The scrambled eggs are burning!" Papá was embarrassed, but Tante Connie just smiled and told him to be quiet and explained that the eggs were not real. I think she secretly enjoyed what he did because she had a very good sense of humor.

Papá also took us to a circus in Vienna where the elephants did tricks and the lions and tigers appeared in the ring. I didn't enjoy the circus, however. I felt sorry for the animals because they were in captivity and kept restrained. Another time he took us into the world-famous amusement park of Vienna, the Prater, where we rode the giant Ferris wheel.[1] The ride from beginning to end took a whole hour. From the highest point I could see all over the city into the countryside along the Danube.

A big change occurred when Papá saw the necessity of sending all of his school-age children to the local schools. Rupert and I had to take the usual tests to be admitted to high school. It was a school for boys and girls, ages twelve to eighteen. The classes for the boys were upstairs, and the classes for the girls, downstairs. We both passed the test, but I was informed that I had to go through another year of elementary school before I could go to the high school because I was too young. Another year of elementary school with Fräulein Freckmann! I was disappointed, but there was nothing I could do. The year went by, and I passed a second test. From then on, Rupert and I went to school together. Hedwig attended a nearby elementary school.

Werner and Maria were sent to the Stiftschule, a Catholic elementary school. Werner had not played with boys his age before; at home he had only one older brother and all those sisters. He did not know how to make friends with the other little boys, so he made up a friend, Severin. He talked to him and about him, but we never saw Severin. I believe Papá would have invited one of the boys from school to play with Werner if he had known of Werner's longing for a friend. It wasn't until much later that we realized this friend was imaginary.

Fräulein Freckmann prepared us well with regard to various academic subjects. She could not, however, prepare us for the transition from a one-on-one learning situation to a classroom with thirty-five pupils and teachers who assumed that Rupert and I had gone through the usual elementary education. We had to make a very difficult adjustment.

When I was twelve years old, Fräulein Freckmann prepared Rupert and me for our first Holy Communion. It was the last thing she did for us before she went home to Germany; her services as governess would no longer be needed when we went to school. A special Mass in the crypt of the church was arranged for the occasion. An Augustinian priest said the Mass, and all the family was present. It was a beautiful celebration during which I was lost in the love of Jesus.

Tante Connie tended to the three little ones—Hedwig, Johanna, and Martina—until soon after the death of Mamá. Then she went to Vienna to be with Gromi, who had been so good to her during World War I. Being up in years, Gromi needed a companion and someone to take care of her apartment. Connie Baby accompanied her mother. Papá then hired a housekeeper by the name of Frau von Klimbacher and a nanny for the little ones.

One day Papá called Rupert and me into the dining room for a conference. He told us that he knew of some beautiful islands from the time he sailed around the world on the *Saida II*. Coconuts and bananas grew in abundance on these Pacific islands, and it was always summer there. Painting a lovely picture for us of these wonderful islands, he said that he would buy a sailboat big enough for the whole family and take us there if we wanted to go. Rupert and I looked at each other, and then Rupert said, "No, we do not want to go there." I agreed, and the matter was closed. Papá did not insist. Later I asked Rupert why he told Papá that we did not want to go there, and he said, "Because there is no Catholic Church there, and we have to go to church on Sunday."

Soon Papá came up with another plan. "Would you like to move to Salzburg? There, two of my officers from the navy are living with their families: Hugo Seiffertitz and Uncle Erwin Wallner." (As you will recall, Erwin had married Tante Lorlein Auersperg.) The plan was met with enthusiasm, not so much because Papá's friends lived there, but because we remembered going to this city with Mamá; she had taken us from the Erlhof to the dentist in Salzburg. On that occasion we had stayed in the hotel Oesterreichischer Hof. We had a room with a balcony from which we could look over the little square in front of the hotel and see what was going on in the street below. A red taxi stood right in the middle of the square. Rupert had been glued to the railing of the balcony, reporting every move the taxi made.

Now, three years after Mamá's passing, Papá intended to move to this wonderful place called Salzburg. We were delighted and ready to move immediately. But we had to wait until a house could be found and the money was available to buy it. Only recently I found out that Tante Nesti bought some of Mamá's property in Fiume so that Papá could afford the house in Salzburg. How Papá found this house that was large enough to hold the family, the staff, and the Stieglers I do not know, but he found one and had it rebuilt for our needs. It was located in Aigen, a beautiful residential area in the country outside Salzburg.

The situation of our new home was not accidental. I believe the Lord had a hand in finding its location. When we had to leave Austria in 1938, after the invasion of the country, all we had to do was to leave by a little gate at the far end of the garden, cross the railroad tracks, and enter the station in order to board the train that would take us south across the border into Italy.

This time it was not winter but summer when we moved, and Papá again arranged for us children to spend the time of the move in Goldegg with our friends and relatives, the Auerspergs. There we had a wonderful time playing croquet and other games. When we left Goldegg, we came into a fully furnished beautiful home, which this time belonged to us. We loved it!

The house was surrounded by a very large garden with big trees, many bushes, and small meadows. When we did not have homework to do, we played in the garden, sometimes far away from the house. We would not have heard anyone calling us. The boatswain's whistle was the answer.

In the movie *The Sound of Music*, the Captain (our father) summons his children with a boatswain's whistle. When we moved to Aigen, Papá began using a whistle to summon his children, and there was a very good reason to do so. The house was large, and our rooms were on the second floor. Papá's study was downstairs. We lived with our doors closed, and Papá never came to our rooms. The sound of the whistle penetrated the wooden doors, whereas his voice would not have reached us. Each one of us had a certain signal, and Papá had a special signal when he called us all together. We loved our signals. Perhaps some of us even imagined that we were sailors on Papá's ship. He did not, however, use the whistle to summon the staff or to place us into formation as shown in the movie.

At the edge of the woods in a meadow, Papá had a little log playhouse built especially for us. It had a door and a bench outside. Again, as in the Martinschlössl, there were small buildings on the

Leiterwagen

premises: a laundry house where two hired women washed all our laundry, a stable, and a little building for garden tools. Again, Franz Stiegler was in charge of the barnyard, and Papá bought two cows for milk. Directly behind our grounds was the railroad station, Aigen bei Salzburg. Though it was a small station, the fast trains stopped there.

In the fall, Papá placed us in the local schools: the girls in the Ursuline Convent school, and the boys in the public school. Since we had no transportation, we walked to and from school, rain or shine. It was three-quarters of an hour each way. Walking was good exercise, yet sometimes the distance seemed awfully long. Later we got bicycles to ride to school—a welcome improvement!

Papá always tried to find something special that would interest us. One day he brought home a dog. It was not just any dog, but a big black Newfoundland of gentle temperament, strong enough to pull a little cart. In Austria the little cart was called *Leiterwagen* (ladder wagon) because all four sides were made of sections like little ladders. Papá showed us how to hitch the dog to our *Leiterwagen* so that one of us could sit in it, usually Martina, being the baby and the lightest one. Our dog was named Gombo.

A neighbor came to Papá one day and told him that our big black dog had been seen chasing deer in the woods. I don't think Papá believed him. But there were more reports, and one of them was that Gombo had killed a deer in the woods. The people who lived in the vicinity insisted that the dog had to be destroyed because he was dangerous. That was the end of Gombo.

One day in the fall, Papá brought two American beehives and had them set up in the garden at the edge of a group of large spruce trees. They were a present from our neighbor, Dachie Preuschen. The hives stood all winter by the spruce trees, and I believe that everyone thought the bees would get along by themselves and produce a lot of honey in the spring and summer.

In the early spring when the snow was melting on the grounds, I wandered over to the beehives. There seemed to be no traffic at the entrance, just a few tired bees, and I looked into the back of the hives. I found dead and moldy bees and watery combs. It did not look as if there was much going on inside the hive.

I told Papá what I had found and asked him whether I could take care of the bees. So Papá went to the headmaster of the local elementary school who was a professional beekeeper. He asked him to come and look over our two beehives and perhaps tell me how to take care of them. Der Herr Oberlehrer brought me a bee hood, gloves, and a smoker. Then he opened the hives, cleaned them out, and found a nucleus of bees and the queen bee intact. He told me how to take care of them by putting a starter comb into the frames. Then he came often to show me other things, such as how to catch a swarm and how to extract honey. That same fall I harvested twelve pounds of dark spruce honey, had a new swarm, and started another hive to house the swarm.

The Bee-House

The next year I had three swarms and needed even more space. So Papá asked Hans Schweiger, our butler and handyman, to build a *Bienenhaus* (bee house) for the hives. He had him place it by the fence along the railroad tracks, away from the general traffic of the family. Eventually I had seven large bee colonies.

Another one of Papá's ideas involved chickens: Why not have a chicken farm on the part of our property that was not used for anything? His good friend Dachie Preuschen brought him plans, showing how to set up an efficient American chicken farm, and Papá and Hans started building the chicken coops according to the plans. Soon the little chicks arrived in boxes by mail, along with feeding troughs and drinking bells. Martina asked, "Where are the little chicks going to grow up until they are big enough to live in the coops?" Papá decided on a large empty room on the third floor that was just the right size.

The Stieglers' living quarters were on the same floor, and Mrs. Stiegler was called upon to help unpack the chicks. It was a great event for all of us when the little yellow peeping feather balls emerged. Mrs. Stiegler was also placed in charge of feeding the chicks and cleaning the area. While they grew quickly under her care upstairs, Papá and Hans were putting the finishing touches on the chicken coops outside, and it wasn't long before the teenage chicks were taken to their new, permanent housing. There were even electric lights in their new home. We gave them special feed to help them produce large eggs with strong shells, and Papá made laying boxes with trap doors so we could identify which hens had laid which eggs. Papá sold the eggs to hotels in Salzburg.

About that time Papá brought home a baby goat. It was pure white, like the chickens, and it was a birthday present for Hedwig. The kid was deposited in the area that had been fenced off for the chickens, so it could not run away. The whole family loved the chickens and the kid.

I remember helping collect the eggs, a job I enjoyed. One day when Papá opened a trap door, he had a surprise. There was the little white kid, struggling to get out of its prison. The goat had seen the hens going into the laying boxes and must have thought it was a hen, too, and could do whatever the hens did. That was the story of the day!

Now that Papá had made a home for his children, he started to sing songs for us that he remembered from his time in the navy. Some of them were the ones his crew made up in order to learn certain commands or the numbers in the German language. Some songs had humorous stanzas. Papá also remembered several funny ballads and other songs from his younger years. He always accompanied these songs with the guitar. Of course, we learned them quickly, just as we had all the other songs we heard.

Papá taught Rupert and Maria the accordion. He taught Johanna the violin, which she eventually played very well. Maria also played the violin. He gave me a small guitar and showed me the chords I needed for accompaniment. We practiced these instruments feverishly until we were able to play marches and folk dances together. Musical evenings became a daily occurrence, and we enjoyed them greatly. Our father played the first violin, Rupert or Maria played the accordion, and I played the accompaniment on the guitar. Later, Johanna joined us playing the second violin. Our little ensemble was now in Viennese terms Ein Schrammel Quartet. The Schrammel Quartet is a Viennese specialty, not of food, but of folk music. It usually consists of one or two violins, an accordion, and one or two guitars. Sometimes a bass fiddle is added. One can hear this music in little restaurants in Grinzing, a suburb of Vienna, during the time of harvest when the new wine is served. This music creates a happy and festive mood. Our Schrammel Quartet, however, was not accompanied by a glass of wine. It was for us, in itself, a wonderful entertainment.

The fact that we children were exposed to music early in our lives and enjoyed and cultivated our musical talents is in direct contrast to the story presented in *The Sound of Music.* In the play and film, it appears that our second mother was solely responsible for teaching us the joys of music. In reality, not only did we play instruments and sing with Papá in the house in Salzburg before we had even met our second mother, but we also sang very early in our lives at the Erlhof during World War I, when Mamá, Gromi, and the aunts sang and played the piano.

I remember one of our first musical adventures away from home. In the summer of 1926, Uncle Karl Auersperg arranged a camping trip for all members of his family who lived in Goldegg, including some members of their staff. He also invited Papá and any of us who might enjoy this venture. The campsite was to be on the floor of a glacier, which had receded and was surrounded by the higher peaks of the mountain range known as Die Niederen Tauern. It was the highest point of the road that ran over this mountain pass, well above the timberline. There the air was cool and clear, incredibly light and clean. The glacier water running through this valley was like crystal, and the morning dew sparkled on the sparse grasses and mountain flora. The atmosphere in those high regions was indescribably beautiful.

There must have been preparations of which we children had no idea. But not long before this expedition started, Papá came home driving a car. He introduced it as "our new car." It was a red Daimler, an open touring car. It had a roof made of canvas, which could be pulled up for protection against rainy weather and folded back for seeing the countryside. It had a rack in back for the luggage. It had to be cranked up in front with a handle to start it. This car was another one of Papá's surprises. From then on, we could drive to Salzburg in five minutes; on a bicycle it still took about a half hour, and on foot, three-quarters of an hour. Soon, however, the Daimler was found to have faulty brakes and had to go back to the factory. As it could not be repaired, the car was exchanged for another one. This car was a beautiful shade of blue and seemed to be in good working order.

It happened that Mamá's brother Franky also lived in our vicinity with his wife, Gretl, and their only son, Johnny. They also joined the camping party. Uncle Franky owned a Tatra, a four-cylinder car with a folding roof like ours.

On the appointed day our new car was packed with luggage, sleeping bags, and provisions. Rupert, Werner, Maria, and I were selected to go along on the trip. We all met at the place chosen for the camp. The men put up the tents, and the ladies made the meals.

Music was the highlight of the trip. Uncle Karl played the accordion—a very complicated instrument with many buttons for both hands, which sounded like a small organ. Papá played the violin, and so did First Lieutenant Pokiser, the tutor of the Auersperg children. I think they traded off playing the first and second violin parts in different pieces. Herr Mastalier, the music teacher of the Auersperg children, played the guitar. A Schrammel Quartet was in session! They played mornings and afternoons. In the evenings when the children and the ladies had retired to their tents, the quartet would walk from tent to tent serenading us. They started to play at quite a distance, and as they came closer to the tents, we had a wonderful feeling as we were surrounded by this lovely music.

Uncle Karl made Hungarian goulash for the whole party of about thirty persons, while the ladies prepared the drinks and the rest of the meal. In the meantime, Lorli Meran, our cousin, then a little girl of about five years of age, wearing a red dirndl and a bright blue apron, went to the brook to watch the fish. Suddenly she felt a pull on her apron from the back. As she turned, she looked right into the face of a cow that was starting to eat her apron strings. Fortunately she was used to animals of all kinds, and she calmly started to pull her apron strings out of the cow's mouth. Only with the help of one of the adults who quickly came to her aid did she recover her apron.

For approximately three weeks we enjoyed an unforgettable family reunion. Then it was time to part, and each family and party went to its respective home. We left the mountains behind. Although we parted from our relatives, we took the music home with us. By that time we knew most of the pieces by heart.

When school started in September, the camping trip faded from our memories, but the music remained and became part of our repertoire. With Rupert on the accordion, Papá on the first violin, Maria on the second violin, and me on the guitar, we made music whenever we could find time!

Our repertoire was enriched, our enthusiasm was stirred, and we played the new pieces that we had heard on the mountain again and again. One of them we called "The Tauern Marsch" (The Tauern March). There were other dance melodies and songs that we loved to play. At that time my father wrote to his cousin Flora in the United States: "My children sing and play music all day long. One does that only when one is young."

8

A New Mother and
Two Baby Sisters

Before Mamá died, she told Papá that he should marry again.
She knew that she was leaving him with seven small
children, the oldest ten and the youngest not yet two. They
needed a mother's love, care, and attention, and so did our big
household.

Around this time, Papá was encouraged to marry a distant relative
of Mamá's—an Austrian countess. This marriage, however, did not
materialize. Papá was too heartsick over the loss of his beloved
Agathe to think of marrying again so soon after her death. He
engaged a housekeeper to oversee the household help and to
supervise the routine of the older children. In Aigen it was Baroness
Rita Mandelsloh, a refined, soft-spoken lady in her sixties, who went
quietly about her duties.

After the scarlet fever epidemic in Klosterneuburg, Maria and
Werner still suffered from the effects of the illness. Both had heart
murmurs and were supposed to be careful not to overexert
themselves. But where does one draw the line? How does one know
what is too much? Maria was given a constant warning: "You must
not do this. You must not do that. This is too much and that is too
much." I believe that her spirit was dampened by being

overprotected, which had an effect opposite from what it was meant to have. Playing the violin was one of the few things she could do that did not carry the warning, "Do not overdo."

In those days, the "little ones" and the "big ones" were strictly separated. The little ones, Hedwig, Johanna, and Martina, had a room together, with the nanny watching over their daily routine. They had a playroom of their own.

The big ones, Rupert, Maria, Werner, and I, had already outgrown a governess. Maria and I had a large room together, with two desks where each of us did homework. The two boys had separate rooms. Baroness Mandelsloh hovered over the whole, big household and family with a motherly attitude. Every night she came to our bedsides to say "good night" and to talk to us or solve any problems we might have. I remember her with great affection. But Baroness Mandelsloh was a housekeeper, not a teacher.

When Maria started having increased fatigue because of her heart condition, Papá became worried. The forty-five-minute walk to and from school, as well as the long day in the classroom, exhausted her. Finally Maria could no longer attend class, and a teacher was needed to tutor her at home so that she would not have to repeat the grade. Papá went to the director of the Ursuline High School to inquire about a student from the higher grades who might live with us and help Maria with her studies. The director knew of no student to fill this role, but he did have the name of a teacher, a postulant at the Nonnberg Abbey, who was qualified and could live in. Her name was Gustl Kutschera, and she was twenty-one years old. The doctor had recommended that this particular teacher should leave the convent for a year and get a job because of constant headaches. He felt that her headaches were caused by the sudden confining life she had to lead in the convent.

Papá hired Gustl on the spot, sight unseen. The next day she reported to our house. Papá called us downstairs with his boatswain's whistle. We came down the wide staircase two by two because it was the fastest way to get down. Then we stood in front of a person whose clothes looked as if they had come from a comic book.

Gustl—Maria Augusta Kutschera was her full name—wore a dark blue summer dress with an unusual neckline, and a leather hat. In one hand she held a briefcase, and in the other hand, a guitar. We greeted her politely, without great enthusiasm, because she would only be the teacher of our sister Maria. She would have nothing to do with the rest of us. After the initial introduction, Gustl was shown to her room and informed of the time and place of the next meal. We children disappeared into our rooms to finish our homework.

During the following days, we did not see much of Gustl, who was spending her time with Maria. Only at mealtimes did she join the family. Little by little she started to talk to all of us, and when she found out that we liked to sing, she joined in our songs. She also taught us folk songs that she knew. What a difference between Gustl and the housekeepers, who were much older than we were and never joined in! At that particular time, Gustl made friends with the rest of us. Because she was interacting with the children to whom she had not been assigned, she was entering into someone else's territory. That created a problem for our Baroness Mandelsloh.

Since there were many hours when Gustl did not have to teach, she was asked to use the time to mend the many stockings of the children. Mending stockings is not common in the United States. But in Austria at that time, the stockings that the young girls wore were made not of silk or nylon, but of a rather heavy cotton knit. When the heels were worn thin, they could be mended and made as good as new. The knee-highs of the boys also needed mending, so there were about fourteen pairs of stockings and thus, twenty-eight single stockings needing work. It took a long time to mend them! Gustl hated the job, but she complied. I can still see her sitting on a cushion on the floor with a mountain of stockings beside her. She moaned and groaned and sighed about what a tedious and hard job it was and that she did not know how to mend.

Finally I offered to help. Now she had a companion in her misery and started to tell me about her childhood in Vienna and her life at the convent. She also wanted to know what I thought about various things. I was thirteen years old then. She told me that she was born on a train going from Tyrol to Vienna. Her mother was traveling home to be with her husband when the baby arrived, but Gustl arrived sooner than was expected. Her mother died soon after her birth, and her father entrusted her to the care of a foster mother who lived on the outskirts of Vienna.

Gustl continued to tell me about her childhood. When she was nine years old, her father died, and a relative, whom she called "Uncle Franz," became her legal guardian. He loved to punish Gustl. For example, on her way home from school, she would stop to pick wildflowers to bring home. Uncle Franz punished her for not coming straight home. He punished her daily, whether she had done something wrong or not. Gustl decided to enjoy herself with her school friends in spite of Uncle Franz's orders because she knew he would punish her anyway.

She told me that she wanted to become a teacher, so she ran away and enrolled in a boarding school that offered a teachers' training course. To pay for her room and board, she did embroidery. During the summer months, she traveled with a youth group of boys and girls known as Neuland. Their purpose was to reform the social order of the day. She was part of their choir and enjoyed going throughout the countryside, giving concerts and collecting folk songs. The young people in the group wore imitation peasant clothing. The girls wore dirndl-like dresses that they made themselves. The boys wore *Lederhosen* and jackets. All of them wore sandals. They despised what they called the "sophisticated society."

Something else Gustl told me about was her love of music. Because she loved music and could not afford to go to concerts, she attended Mass in the Catholic churches in Vienna on Sundays. Her purpose was not to worship, but to hear the music that did not cost anything. One day she heard a sermon, and after Mass, she sought out the priest. She poured out to him all her opposition to and resentment of the Catholic Church. He listened until she finished talking and said, "Kneel down and confess your sins." In that moment she said that she changed. The next time they had Mass in the school chapel she went forward to take Holy Communion to demonstrate her conversion. She was then sorry that she had previously convinced her classmates to turn away from the Catholic Church and tried to change their unbelief.

Sometime after her conversion Gustl went mountain climbing with some friends. On top of a mountain, seeing the surrounding beauty, she made a sudden decision to give up all this earthly beauty and enter a convent. Looking for the strictest one, she entered the Benedictine order in Salzburg. She described her misbehavior there and the patience of the nuns as they caught her sliding down banisters, singing and whistling in the corridors, and coming late for prayers. Finding a way to go up to a flat part of the roof, she looked out over the town of Salzburg and passed her free time reading. The song titled "How Do You Solve a Problem Like Maria?" from *The Sound of Music* was very appropriate.

During our mending sessions, Gustl also told me another interesting story. At one time, before she came to our home, she had seen us walking two by two with Fräulein Freckmann in Klosterneuburg. She said, "When I saw how she had you walking in such a regimented way, I really felt sorry for you children. I would have liked to have been your governess then."

I wondered how she knew it had been us and how she knew Fräulein Freckmann by name. She told me that she used to visit the lady in whose house the seminars on early Christian liturgy were held. She had met Fräulein Freckmann there. Was that a coincidence? Because of her interesting stories, our time mending passed quickly.

She intensely disliked Baroness Mandelsloh, and the feeling was mutual. Baroness Mandelsloh saw her as an intruder, and Gustl saw Baroness Mandelsloh as a necessary evil. Baroness Rita Mandelsloh retreated from the situation and took her leave. There was only one more thorn in Gustl's side: Frau Stiegler. She had adored Mamá and resented Gustl's intrusion, but Frau Stiegler stayed.

Papá had become fond of Gustl when he saw that she was interested in his children and that we all responded well to her. We were busy learning new songs, playing volleyball, and hiking into the mountains with her.

Mr. Hankey, an American who owned a yacht in Bremerhaven, Germany, wrote Papá a letter. He asked Papá to consider sailing this yacht from Bremerhaven to Genoa, Italy, as a hired captain. Papá became interested in this venture since sailing was his specialty. He also saw it as a way to enjoy being at sea again, using his skills of sailing unfamiliar waters. This request presented a wonderful challenge for him, and with everything at home going well, he took the job.

After several weeks he was back home, having accomplished his mission to the satisfaction of Mr. Hankey. One day Papá asked me into his study. He sat down on the sofa, and I sat in a chair next to him. He asked, "Do you think I should marry Gustl? You know, she's quite pretty." I remember the exact words of my answer to Papá: "I think if it is the will of God, then you should marry her." At the age of fourteen this was not my usual way of thinking, but the words just flowed out. Papá may have asked some of the other children too.

On November 27, 1927, Papá married Gustl in the Church of the

Nonnberg Abbey. Now Papá had a second wife, and we seven had a second mother. Immediately after the wedding, the question arose of how we should address her as our new mother. Gustl sensed this delicate question had to be settled. She said to us, "Why don't you call me 'Mother'? That distinguishes me from your real mother, and at the same time, it is appropriate because I am now your mother."

At first it was a little difficult and awkward to use a name we had never used before, but eventually we became accustomed to it. We did not realize then that we would be cemented together with this new mother for the next twenty-nine years in a musical adventure that would save us from the terrifying upheaval of World War II and would take us across the ocean to a new continent, which was to become our new home: America.

Gustl was twenty-two years of age and Papá was forty-seven when she married into our family. She was only six years older than Rupert, the oldest son, and eight years older than I was. She knew much more of the world outside the confines of our home than we did due to the circumstances of her childhood and schooling. She had definite opinions about life and voiced them "loud and clear." Now that she was our second mother and we were her obedient children, she slowly became the important person in our lives.

Mother was young and full of energy. She perceived our well-regulated daily routine as boring and lifeless and wanted to bring fun and more pleasant activities into our lives. She disliked the fact that it took us so-o-o long to do our homework but did enjoy Papá's after-dinner "coffee hour." It was Papá's special time with us. He had our butler, Hans, bring into the living room a set of demitasse cups made of rice china, which he had bought in the Middle East during his trip around the world. These cups and a copper pot with a wooden handle were set up on an ornate oriental brass tray. Papá added a spoonful of sugar to the water in the copper pot and brought it to the boiling point over a small flame. Then he added the coffee, which he ground in a hand grinder, to the boiling water. This was the daily social hour before we went to our different activities after lunch or dinner. I believe that Papá really relished this moment when all our eyes were glued to his hands. After handing each one of his children a cup filled with this delicious brew, he started telling us stories from his early life. I still treasure those hours with Papá and his Turkish after-dinner coffee. They were very special moments.

During the years that followed the wedding, our new mother made many changes in our family. She changed the way we dressed, what we ate, and how we lived. A new wind blew through our house. She was apprehensive about being a second mother; therefore, she read many books about how to be a stepmother and how children react to second mothers. Her readings suggested that children often do not accept a stepmother. That, however, was not the case in our family; we accepted her completely. Because of her readings to the contrary, she did not believe our acceptance, a misperception on her part that would lead to many future misunderstandings.

Our new mother thought of numerous things for us to do. We continued to participate in all the activities she liked so much and had introduced to us before she married Papá. Mother was fond of volleyball, so we played with her for hours. I hated volleyball! She loved mountain climbing, so the whole family went mountain climbing in the summer and during the school year.

She organized our free time with other outdoor activities, such as bicycle trips. She taught us ancient dances, which she had learned in her youth group, and we danced them on our lawn. Evenings were taken up with singing. All of these activities had been part of her earlier life, and we enjoyed them because they were new and entertaining.

Sometimes these activities collided with homework. By that time, my sister Maria had recovered enough to resume her school schedule, so all of us had homework. Even though we enjoyed the new activities Mother planned for us, especially the mountain climbing, there was always the question: How are we going to finish our homework? This especially created a dilemma for me because I was very conscientious about my lessons. Although Mother loved creating free-time activities for us, she hated housework and was glad that there was a staff to do it.

Mother was a wonderful storyteller. Whenever she would tell a story, I would become so fascinated that I would stare at her continuously in order to watch her expressions. This continual staring made her very uncomfortable, and she let me know it in no uncertain terms. I, however, misinterpreted her dislike of my staring at her and thought she did not like my face.

Mother had an overwhelming personality that drew people to her like a magnet. Today, we would say she had charisma. In turn, she adored being the center of attention. This was so much the case that, as the years passed, Papá became more withdrawn and seemed to fade into the background.

Mother had many strong opinions, and soon she tried to convince us that a reform of the existing lifestyle of our society was necessary. For instance, she did not approve of drinking alcohol or smoking. Since the adverse health effects of these activities were not known at the time, her objections were purely on a personal basis.

Because she had attended a school that embraced a socialistic ideology, with which she agreed, she had strong prejudices against the aristocracy. She stated that this class of people was "degenerate." These beliefs created confusion among us older children since our own relatives were solid, down-to-earth people who lived simple lives, in spite of the fact that they owned and lived in castles. I could not understand why she thought that my relatives needed to be reformed. Mother had such strong ideas that it was useless to object or argue with her.

Papá, in his quiet way, tried to steer her away from these ideas by introducing her to Mamá's cousins and their families who lived in the vicinity of Salzburg. Imagine her surprise when she discovered that "those aristocrats" were intelligent, kind, warmhearted people, who each had a wonderful sense of humor and did not live glamorous or overindulgent lives as she had imagined! She learned a lot from them, and later in life, she would use the title of "Baroness" herself!

Mother had to learn how to be a parent in a large family whose background was very different from hers, just as we had to adjust to a personality different from anyone we had ever met.

In February 1929, there was the excitement of a new baby in the family. The sweet new baby was named Rosmarie. She had blonde curls and dark eyes. Two years later another baby girl was born. We named her Eleonore, but we called her "Lorli." Lorli had dark brown curls and very dark eyes. She was the admiration of all who laid eyes on her. We loved and admired both of our new baby sisters. Hedwig, age fourteen, became their nanny under Mother's supervision. Our two baby sisters had a room together and their own routines. However, there was a big difference; Rosmarie and Lorli were not confined to the nursery the way our "little ones" had been.

Now Mother had to adjust not only to her new ready-made family, but also to new infants of her own. That, together with the new lifestyle, new relatives, and new responsibilities such as housekeeping, made her days very busy.

These were only the first changes introduced by our new mother. Before us lay dramatic changes that neither she, nor Papá, nor any of us could foresee.

9

Spreading My Wings

I did not see much of my little sisters since I was so busy studying for my high school graduation. In the spring of 1931, Rupert and I graduated from high school. I had studied in Salzburg at a girls' school, Mädchen Reform Real Gymnasium, while Rupert attended a Benedictine boarding school for boys near Vienna. There was no special celebration to mark our graduation, but Papá arranged a surprise for us. He thought our horizons would be widened with a summer trip to England to visit our British relatives, Mamá's family. Our great-uncle, Bertie Whitehead, and his wife, Rosie, lived in a beautiful manor house in southern England.

Together, Rupert and I ventured out into the big, wide world. We traveled by train and boat, of course. Rupert had always been interested in everything about trains. He knew exactly what to do and when to do it, from changing trains to deciphering schedules.

From Salzburg we traveled to Cologne, Germany, arriving at midnight. There we had to wait two hours for the next train to Bremen. I suggested that we tour the town to pass the time, so we set out in the dimly lit streets to have a look at the famous cathedral of Cologne. As we wandered around, we saw a vendor of potato pancakes on the side of the street. He fried a huge, round pancake on a little pot-bellied stove. That golden-brown pancake was the only bright spot in the dark city!

From Cologne, we went on to Bremen, where we boarded the boat. When we arrived in England, Rupert found our way to the train station. From the moment we stepped aboard the train in England, we felt the hospitality and the kindness of the railroad personnel. We felt as if we were guests of the railroad, not passengers. That was different from our experiences on the European trains. The English conductor was polite and personable, and although we were not traveling first class, we felt that we were. As the English countryside rolled by, tables were unfolded so the passengers could play games or cards. Before we arrived in London, we were served tea with little biscuits.

Uncle Bertie Whitehead, our grandfather's brother, met us at the station in London. He was a heavy-set, white-haired man with a kindly look about him. Rupert and I saw glimpses of the great city of London as Uncle Bertie drove us to his estate in Dorset. Aunt Rosie greeted us warmly and showed us to our rooms. To our great surprise and joy, there was our former maid from Austria, Hanni! She now worked for the Whiteheads. Her presence made us feel at home in the house of our English relatives whom we were meeting for the first time. Despite the adventure of traveling alone, Rupert and I were still rather shy.

Uncle Bertie rented bicycles for us, so we would be somewhat independent. This part of England had rolling grasslands, and we enjoyed cycling through the countryside with its long hedges that divided the pastures. Perhaps to give us something constructive to do, Uncle Bertie arranged for us to take typing lessons in a neighboring town.

Rupert and I saw more of England when Uncle Bertie drove us through the countryside. His brother, Bede, was no longer living, but Uncle Bertie took us to his nearby estate anyway. Uncle Bede's widow still lived there with their son. They invited us to have English tea with them, and then they arranged for their forester to give us a tour through their extensive woodlands.

The forester was an experienced woodsman, who knew exactly what the birds and animals "said" and did. He explained the various birdcalls and demonstrated some of them on a little whistle. As we walked through the brush and woodlands, he suddenly stood still and said, "There is a weasel around here somewhere who is after a rabbit!" How did he know that? The forester told us that the birds "said" it. We saw nothing, but then, after a few minutes, sure enough, the rabbit came running, with the weasel in pursuit. So intent was the weasel on its prey that he didn't notice us until the forester went after him with a branch. The kindhearted forester did not want Rupert and me to witness a battle between the rabbit and the weasel. The weasel left the scene in a hurry! I recall that walk in the woods as a highlight of our English visit.

Uncle Bertie was determined that we should see the two famous images cut into the hillsides by Phoenicians thousands of years ago. One was the shape of a goat; the other was the shape of a giant. Since the hills were of pure white limestone, overgrown with grass, these white cutouts shone far out into the nearby sea. Uncle Bertie told us that these images had been landmarks for ancient seafarers, in the same way lighthouses on the coasts of Europe and America were used.

We saw the rosy-purple fields of English heather in a place named New Forest. What a breathtaking sight! The New Forest was simply a vast area of blooming heather, with clusters of oaks here and there. There was much wildlife in this natural setting; as we drove through the area, we saw wild ponies peacefully grazing beside the road.

As the sun slowly set in the west, Uncle Bertie drove us up a gently sloping hill toward Stonehenge. There, with a setting sun and a fiery red sky as a backdrop, stood the age-old stone circle of rocks. Rupert and I were awestruck, but Uncle Bertie explained in a perfectly matter-of-fact voice, "No one really knows what Stonehenge is. Some say it is a pagan site for human sacrifice; others say that it is an ancient calendar constructed by the Druids. But actually no one can tell with certainty why it was built."

The site is a complete mystery. It is unknown how the huge stones were brought to this spot; this type of rock is not native to the area. Uncle Bertie speculated that the stones had been brought by sea.

Rupert and I, however, wondered how such weight could have been transported, given the primitive technology of ancient times. No matter how or why Stonehenge came into being, it seemed to me totally awesome as we stood gazing in wonder. Even after all these years, Stonehenge is still a fascinating puzzle to me.

When Rupert and I returned to Salzburg after our trip, it was time to make decisions about the upcoming school year. Rupert entered the University of Innsbruck. First, he studied for a career in business, which was Papá's wish. He later switched to his real interest, medicine.

One day Mother took me aside and bombarded me with questions about what I wanted to do with my life. I was really bewildered by her questions. I felt that she wanted me to make a sudden decision about my future without any guidance. I was not prepared to do that, so the moment was very painful for me. It had never dawned on me that I might be expected to leave my home for a career. I liked languages and art, but how could I make a profession of those interests, especially since I had little experience or knowledge of the outside world?

Before long, Mother made the decision for me. Since she thought I had a talent for languages, she arranged for me to go to France as an exchange student. I was actually looking forward to my visit to France. I already knew a little French and liked the language. However, shortly before my departure date, we were informed that plans had changed, and the French family could not have me visit.

Since languages seemed to be the way to go, Mother suggested an English interpreter's course for me. I had always been interested in the English language and was familiar with it from childhood because I had heard English spoken at the Erlhof. I pursued this course in Salzburg, passing with excellent grades. Immediately following this, I was offered a job of teaching English in the same high school from which I had graduated. That prospect scared me. I did not feel like going back into a classroom. I was sure I would become tongue-tied in front of a class of young girls, so I decided against this position. I never told anyone about this offer and never requested my diploma from the interpreter course. My reasoning was that if Mother knew I had the diploma along with this job offer, she would pressure me into taking the teaching job. I felt that I did not have the training to be a teacher. Besides, I was so shy that I knew I would not be able to communicate in a classroom situation.

Mother arranged to have me tutor the daughter of our next-door neighbor because I could not think of an alternative. This fourteen-year-old girl, Minki, had broken her leg in a skiing accident. Her parents were very wealthy, and Minki's mother was going to Africa on a safari. She was leaving her two daughters, ages fourteen and sixteen, in their country villa with the chauffeur and their cook in charge of the household. I was to live there. I was not enthusiastic about this assignment, but was given no choice.

During my time there, Minki was sent to the hospital in Vienna because her leg needed to be in traction. I was to go with her and tutor her in the hospital room. Some of Mamá's relatives, who lived in Vienna, provided me with room and board.

While in Vienna, I visited Gromi in Klosterneuburg, which was about a half-hour train ride followed by a twenty-minute uphill walk. When I arrived at Gromi's house, Uncle Bobby's wife was also there. The three of us had tea together. I was too shy to enter into the conversation, but I was happy to see Gromi again.

The remainder of this school year was spent trying to teach Minki all of her school subjects. I did my best, but she had become uncooperative when she realized I did not have enough knowledge for the job. At age eighteen, I returned home.

Back at home, I had an idea of what I could do next. I loved to sew but needed further instruction. Mother enrolled me in classes at the Salzburg Home Economics School. There I learned to make patterns for a variety of clothing, including dirndl costumes, which we wore. At that time I had no idea that what I was learning would become very useful in later life. That training enabled me to sew and make clothing for us girls for many years to come, including some of the dresses we wore on stage.

Another one of my interests was drawing and painting. Papá had always tried to encourage us to develop our talents. While I was still in high school, and Papá realized that I liked to draw, he engaged an Italian watercolor artist to give me private lessons. The artist, Mr. Susat, came to our home, bringing along the materials I needed to get started. Being very eager to begin the lessons, I learned how to use a pencil for sketching and to use watercolors effectively.

After a few months, Mr. Susat asked me to stop by his house on my way home from school, to pick up a brush that he had bought for me. When I told Papá that I was to stop at my teacher's home for the brush, Papá said that I was not to do so. Feeling that it was an improper suggestion by Mr. Susat, Papá dismissed him. I am sure that Mr. Susat had nothing improper in mind and only wanted to give me the brush, but Papá was very protective of his daughters. Then I was on my own concerning artistic endeavors. I had a good foundation, however, and I am very grateful to Mr. Susat for his substantial teaching, which developed into a lifelong avocation.

One day Mother gave me a book about Chinese brush painting. I was impressed by the fact that Chinese teachers would not allow their pupils to paint for twelve years until they had trained their eyes and their powers of observation. In order to imprint on their minds the shapes and outlines of objects worthy of being painted, they had to study without using a brush. After this training, they were finally taught the art of brush painting.

When I read of this method, I thought, *This is what I will do*, and thus began an everyday habit and my own art technique. Mother suggested that I should spend five minutes drawing a sketch in my book every time I saw something I liked. Sketches of trees, flowers, churches, landscapes, and of my brothers and sisters filled my books. Later on, still relying on Mr. Susat's instruction, I reworked some of my sketches into watercolors.

Years later, when we were on tour in the United States, we were invited to visit a kindergarten. The teacher showed us some of the children's artwork. I was especially impressed by the linoleum block prints the children had made, and I thought: *If these little children can do this, so can I.* I bought the materials I needed and started to cut linoleum blocks and print the design on tissue paper. Later, using art paper, I made Christmas and greeting cards.

When I ran out of ideas for block printing, I went back to my first love—watercolors—and behold! After my first try, all the instructions of Mr. Susat returned. I painted one watercolor after another. I painted landscapes, still lifes, flowers, and buildings. Sketching, painting, and linoleum block printing became my recreation. I did all these things because I enjoyed doing them.

Although I did not realize it at the time, the lessons I received in art, as well as the courses that I took in English and sewing, were to become an excellent preparation for my future.

10

Adventures with Papá

*P*apá was an enthusiastic and experienced sailor. During his years in the navy, he went sailing whenever he had free time, even taking his mother out on a sailboat to give her the benefit of the healthy sea air. When Papá considered us old enough to enjoy a cruise, he decided to give us a special vacation in the summer of 1932.

Since Italy had finally canceled the black list, it was safe for Papá to return to his "old territory," which he had called home for most of his life. His plan was to sail along the coast of the Adriatic Sea to introduce us to the area where he had lived since his childhood and where he had spent time when he was in the navy.

The type of vessel that Papá decided to rent for this voyage was a *Trabakel*. It was a primitive, native cargo vessel, dating back to ancient times, heavily built and decorated on the upper part of the hull with stripes of bright colors. The large sails were mostly bright red, orange, or yellow. The black hull was wide and roomy inside. Some *Trabakels* had been transformed into tourist sightseeing boats for the warm summer months and could be rented for any length of time. Papá hired the *Archimede*, complete with an Italian-speaking crew, consisting of the captain, a sailor, and a cook we called "Cogo," who doubled as a sailor.

A Trabakel

We anticipated this coming vacation with enthusiasm. It was going to be a wonderful summer, full of adventure and beautiful sights to see. The plan was to board the *Archimede* in Trieste, cruise down the coast, visit Venice, and then return to Trieste. There we would take à train to Pola and spend a few weeks camping on an island before going back home.

Our two little ones, Rosmarie and Lorli, were left at home in the care of a nanny so that Mother could come with us. A young woman and family friend, Renate Ross, and a seventeen-year-old boy, Peter Hanns Paumgartner, were invited to join us. Papá gladly added these two to his already large family; our group totaled eleven. Peter's father was the director of the Academy of Music in Salzburg. Peter had studied Italian in school, and his father hoped that the trip would give him a chance to practice his newly acquired language. Peter was exceptionally tall and thin with a pale complexion. In order to avoid sunburn, he wore a white linen hat with an unusually wide brim. He was good-natured, but quite awkward. It seemed that he was not yet able to coordinate his long, thin arms and legs. Among ourselves, we called him the "the Praying Mantis."

Since summer in the Adriatic Sea is warm with little rain, there was no need to take a lot of clothing. We packed our sleeping bags, hammocks, cooking utensils, folding boats,[1] and a change of clothing for sightseeing and church. With our knapsacks on our backs, we headed for the train station, which was just opposite our property in Aigen.

The train took us to Trieste, where we boarded the *Archimede.* Thus, our adventure began. The red sails went up, and the proud symbol of our commandant unfolded. As I look back, these symbols remind me of the Pennsylvania "hex signs." Slowly the vessel moved away from the pier as we headed out to sea. The crew was introduced to us, and throughout the trip, they assumed a kind, fatherly attitude toward their passengers—us. We were shown our "bedroom" below in the large, empty hull. We hung our hammocks and left our knapsacks under them, but we never actually slept there. We girls changed into our training suits, which consisted of long, loose-fitting pants made of dark blue cotton knit and blouses with long sleeves and collars made of the same material. These outfits were similar to the sportswear of today. The boys wore shorts and white shirts, their regular summer outfits.

The deck of the vessel was large. As long as we stayed clear of the ropes, we were permitted to place our sleeping bags wherever we wanted and move freely about the ship. At first our only occupation was to look: look here, look there, look everywhere. As we headed south, the land lay on our left, and the sea stretched out on our right. Little fishing villages came into view, allowing us to hear soft sounds drifting over from the land. It was a new feeling for me to be gliding over the water in this open boat, which was larger than any boat I had been on before. The air was fresh and clear with the scent of the sea.

The nights were warm and balmy, so we slept on deck in our sleeping bags rather than in the musty-smelling hull below. On deck we could see the stars in the dark southern sky twinkling brightly. The moon presided over the entire scene. I could hear the ripple of the waves as they lapped against the sides of the boat, making their own music.

Morning arrived and with it a cup of hot coffee with sugar and condensed milk and a hard sea biscuit handed out by Cogo. As the new day began, Mother was sorting out maps, brochures, and books about all the worthwhile sights, ancient buildings, and museums that we could visit. Mother thought that this vacation trip should add to our education. Personally, I knew I would enjoy seeing the remnants of the ancient Roman civilization about which I had studied in high school.

Whenever we went on land, our new mother bought fruits and wonderful, fresh Italian bread to enhance our meals. While Mother was busy shopping, Peter Hanns was trying to communicate with the crew using the Italian he had learned in school. To his amazement, he found that they did not understand him because they spoke a local Italian dialect, which was not what he had learned.

One beautiful summer afternoon when we were all standing on the deck admiring the sea with its little ripples glistening in the sun, someone called out, "Man overboard!" Peter Hanns's white hat could be seen floating on the water far behind our ship. Papá asked the commandant to turn the ship around because someone had fallen overboard. Since the commandant did not know how to manage this maneuver, Papá quickly took over the ship, and with full sails he turned, sailing toward the white hat. Peter Hanns was rescued and pulled back on deck. He did not know how he had suddenly landed in the water. It was a good thing that he always wore his white hat with the large brim. This time it had saved his life.

Soon after the rescue of Peter Hanns, we anchored in the harbor of Zara, the city where Papá had been born. An account of what happened there, according to my sister Maria's memories, follows:

We noticed a small white house on the shore. In front of the house, a little yacht lay safely behind a wharf, which protected it from the oncoming sea. A brilliant idea came to Mother's mind. "Why don't we rent this house for the winter?" she said, not even knowing if it was for rent. So Papá and Mother took the dinghy from the Archimede and rowed over to the house. They knocked on the door, and a lady answered who was astonished to see two strangers. Papá knew Italian and asked if he could rent the house for the winter. This took the lady by surprise, and she answered, "No, I'm sorry, it is not for rent." I am not sure of the exact conversation that followed, but Mother probably used her charm. After the woman consulted with her family, she came out and told Papá, "Yes, we decided that you may rent the house for the winter." So it happened that we would return there that September.

We then left the harbor of Zara to continue south. Later that same day, we were all standing on the deck, and Papá spied an unusual object in the distance. It turned out to be a folding boat, paddled by two men heading south. Papá knew they were heading for trouble; if they were to continue in that direction crossing the Albanian border, they were at risk of being arrested and imprisoned as spies. Another danger was the coast that had sharp rock formations, some of which were hidden just below the surface of the water. A folding boat could easily be punctured.

Papá gestured for them to steer over to our ship. They understood, and after they came alongside, Papá invited them on board. He discovered that they were students from Oxford, England, who were on an excursion to Greece. They thought that going in a folding boat would be economical and enjoyable. They had no idea of the dangers that awaited them. Papá found that they had no knowledge of the Greek language or the other languages they would need as they traveled south. They told Papá, "If you speak English clearly and distinctly, you will be understood everywhere." This misconception has remained a joke in our family ever since. Papá invited them to bring their folding boat onto the deck of the *Archimede* and join our group as far as Venice. They accepted the invitation gratefully. Our group of passengers was now thirteen!

After the English students were on board, we continued to the Bocche di Cattaro, the most southern port of Austria before World

War I. We anchored for the night, planning to head for Venice the next morning. I looked forward to seeing this famous city.

As we were approaching Venice, a heavy storm came up. The wind increased; the white caps lay in front of the *Archimede*, and its bow rose and sank with the waves. It was the first storm we had encountered on our trip. We neared Venice at sunset, and the skyline was shrouded in mist. We could see the spires, domes, and buildings as if through a thin veil. This sight immediately transported me into the atmosphere of a fairyland.

We arrived in Venice a bit shaken but intact. Although we were ready to walk on firm ground again, this was difficult, for there is little firm ground in Venice and the streets are mostly waterways. As the *Archimede* lay alongside the pier, she was tied loosely because of the waves. She came close to the pier as the waves pushed her there. Then the waves moved her away. Back and forth she went in a constant rhythm. In order to disembark, one had to step from the rim of the deck directly onto the pier. One had to decide exactly the right moment to step over before the ship moved away from the pier.

When I looked down, I could see the water. It was not at all like the mountain lakes in the Alps but more like a liquid garbage dump, filled with melon rinds and other items that had been tossed there. When it was my turn to jump from the ship to the pier, I jumped just a split second too late and, of course, I landed not on the pier but in the liquid garbage dump! I found myself deep down between the hull of the ship and the wall of the pier. My good Sunday dress and my shoes were soaked with horrible-smelling water, making me unfit to go on land. The members of the crew pulled me out, and I had to change my clothes and jump to the pier again. This time I made it!

To go anywhere in Venice, one took a gondola. The gondolier stood in the back, maneuvering the boat with a single long oar, operating it with great skill. He knew every canal. Being very proud of Venice, he acted as a representative of his city and told of its history.

Sightseeing in Venice was truly worthwhile. I marveled at the unique buildings that actually stood in the water. We saw the famous

Cathedral of San Marco and fed the pigeons on the square in front of the cathedral. The square was lined with all kinds of shops to entice tourists to buy a souvenir or two. The glass factory on the Isle of Murano especially impressed me. I watched the glass being blown by methods that were centuries old.

As soon as dusk set in, the city changed. Lights appeared along the canals. One could hear music and gondoliers calling to each other. Forgotten were the melon rinds and the dirty water. One could only feel the mysterious atmosphere that pervaded the evenings. Venice then became a place of song, romance, and poetry.

At the end of our sightseeing, we said good-bye to our friends from England and boarded the *Archimede* for the last time. The students sent us a nice letter of thanks from England. In Trieste we bade farewell to our wonderful crew and took the train to Pola, where our camping equipment was waiting for us at the freight station. The rest of the summer vacation passed quickly. We camped for a few weeks on the island of Veruda before returning home to Aigen with a wealth of beautiful memories that have lasted a lifetime.

We were home just long enough to reunite with the two little ones, hire two teachers and a nanny, and get ready for our trip to Zara that September, back to the white house that Papá had rented for the winter. At this point I am relating an experience that my sister Maria still remembers in detail. The following adventure took place in December of 1932:

The small yacht, *Alba Maris*, came with the house in Zara. The yacht could only sleep four people, so Papá divided us into groups to take us on trips. I was chosen for the crew with Papá, Mother, and Martina. We left in the afternoon and arrived in a beautiful bay to spend the night. Martina, who was eleven years old at the time, made sketches of the scenery. The next morning, looking forward to what the day would bring, we hoisted the anchor and raised the sails. It did not take long before we sighted a Yugoslavian patrol boat, which was heading toward us. Coming alongside the *Alba Maris*, the Yugoslavian patrol officers boarded and asked for our passports.

They also asked many questions. At that time Zara was an Italian free port surrounded by Yugoslavia, with some of the surrounding sea being Italian and the rest being Yugoslavian. Since we were already in Yugoslavian waters, these officers had the right to inspect us. When the officers heard us speaking German, they became very friendly. Their tone, however, changed once they saw our Italian passports.

Since Papá was a citizen of Trieste, which belonged to Austria before the First World War, and was given to Italy afterward, our family woke up one day and discovered that we had become Italian citizens! The Yugoslav patrolmen thought that Papá was a spy, using his family as a camouflage. When they saw the camera, they wanted to know if any photographs had been taken, to which Papá answered, "No." The patrolmen then opened the camera to see if Papá had told the truth. Although they were satisfied that no photos had been taken, Martina's sketches had aroused suspicion. Therefore they decided that the family had to follow them to their Main Station, which was on an island right across the water from Zara.

Two soldiers with bayonets were ordered to come on board the boat in order to take Martina, Mother, Papá, and me to the village dock where the patrol station was. Wanting to show the patrol that we were not afraid, Mother, Martina, and I started to sing, but we were soon told to be quiet because the mayor of the village had died. On the boat, the two soldiers with bayonets watched over our sleeping family, making sure we did not escape. The next morning, we were all taken to the main patrol station. Papá was told to follow the soldiers. We did not know where they had taken him.

Mother summoned all her courage and, with the little Italian she knew, persuaded one of the soldiers to take her to where Papá was. Later, Mother gave us an account of what happened next. After much discussion with Mother, the official put on his cape and white gloves, and tried to lock her in a room. Mother, however, quickly put her foot between the door and the doorframe so he could not close the door. Then she acted as though she was very frightened, arousing his protective instincts. He finally took her to the prison and what did she see? Papá was calmly playing cards with the only other inmate—a murderer!

Finally Papá was freed and the patrol officers led him back to the

Alba Maris. We were very glad to see him! But the ordeal was not yet over. The Yugoslavian officers wanted Papá to go back to the patrol station to sign a paper. Certain that this was a trick, Papá told them to bring the paper to the boat. Miraculously they did! At this point, we were allowed to leave. I was the mechanic on board and tried to crank the engine, but it would not start. Again and again I tried. Finally after a few tries it started and we left the harbor. The mystery of the troublesome engine later became clear; Papá had put new filters in, but had forgotten to perforate them to let the fuel flow through. Little by little, we finally made it home. Of course, at the time the rest of the family at the house in Zara had no idea of what had happened.

Thus ended Maria's account of their adventure.

While Papá, Mother, Maria, and Martina had their encounter with the Yugoslavian border patrol, I was at the house with Hedwig, Johanna, Rupert, Werner, Rosmarie, Lorli, the nanny, and the two teachers. It was Christmas Eve, and I was baking cookies. Earlier we had played Christmas carols on the record player. As the day went on and Papá and his crew did not come back as expected, we wondered what could have happened. We started to pray for their safety. There was nothing else we could do. Finally, to our great relief, we spotted the *Alba Maris* in the distance.

Upon their return to the house, we heard the whole hair-raising story. We then sang "Now Thank We All Our God." After all this excitement, we had a wonderful Christmas together and remained in the rented house in Zara until April, at which time we returned to Aigen. We did not stay at home in Aigen for long. Soon Papá had an idea for another adventure.

In Salzburg the annual summer music festival brought music lovers and performers from all over the world. For two months, every July and August, music enthusiasts streamed into the city, and the hotels and guest houses were filled to the brim. Some visitors looked for large homes to rent where they could stay and entertain guests. Our house in Aigen, outside Salzburg, was perfect for this purpose.

During the summer of 1933, Papá decided to rent our house, with our servants included, to guests of the festival. The renters turned out to be the owners of the Weyerhaeuser Lumber Company of the United States. So where would our family go? It was a time of peace in Europe. Papá was lured by the thought of camping with us on the island of Veruda, off the coast of Italy in the Adriatic Sea.

Veruda was part of the territory that Papá knew so well from his younger years. Along the coast of the Adriatic Sea are strewn cities and towns dating back to the Roman Empire. In Pola, now Croatian but formerly an Austrian harbor, one can still find a well-preserved stadium and other ruins from Roman times.

In this mixture of cultures and population, Papá grew up. Fifteen years earlier, he had lived and worked there to defend his country. He had become acquainted with the local Italian dialect and native way of living. This area had changed after World War I, but the memory of a land of unique beauty remained. Papá remembered the blue skies and soft breezes from the south and the sweet fragrance of aromatic shrubs and herbs brought out by the noontime heat. He yearned to show all of us this wonderful place that he loved so much—the memories of which he silently carried in his heart. He arranged with his friend Mr. Pauletta, who owned a hardware store in Pola, for us to camp on his island, Veruda.

Papá had ordered tents, hammocks, and two folding boats from his cousin, who owned a tent and boating factory in Bavaria. Papá specified that the boats were to be made exceptionally strong; the rubberized canvas was to be seven times stronger than usual. Each boat was equipped with two sails, two paddles, seats for two, and a rudder.

When we were properly outfitted for our trip, Papá shipped our gear by train to Pola. He followed by car with our baggage, and the rest of us took the train to Pola. When we arrived, we went by rowboat the short distance to the island of Veruda.

The family—two parents and nine children—made quite a procession when we arrived with all of our camping gear. We settled on the south side of the island near a cluster of young pines, setting up our tents, hammocks, sleeping bags, and other camping equipment. This part of the island sloped down toward sea level. The entire hill was overgrown with small bushes, which the local people called "bosco." Small as they were, the pines gave enough shade to protect us from the merciless midday sun.

Camp life was not a new experience for us, but camping on an island was. The only way to reach it was by boat. We could walk the circumference of the island in an hour, yet we did not feel confined there. Years before, Rupert and I had imagined living on an island and had wanted to build a raft. Now, the idea of life on an island became a reality for our family, at least for a few weeks!

In the northern part of Veruda high cliffs rose out of the sea. Only one water hole escaped from the ever-pounding surf upon the rocks, which made it perfect for swimming and diving. This spot, elevated high above the sea, gave us a magnificent view of the site that the monks had chosen for their monastery years ago. From its ruins, Mr. Pauletta built a summer cottage for his family. His wife and two daughters came there occasionally during the hottest summer days. Mrs. Pauletta once invited us to an Italian meal in their cottage. She not only cooked it but also, at Mother's request, showed us how to make special fish dishes.

At night we gazed at the stars from our hammocks and listened to the waves lazily lapping the shore. From the sea came the smell of seaweed drying in the sandy bays. Way out at sea, fishermen's songs drifted into our sleepy ears.

In the early morning hours, a voice came across the bay. "Lattee-e-e-e . . . Lattee-e-e-e," it called. Then "Pesch-e-e" and "Calamari . . ." Papá signaled that he wanted to buy milk and occasionally a fresh fish.

For all other commodities, we had to go by boat across the water. When we reached the land, we walked or rode our bicycles into Pola. On Sundays the family went to church there. Afterward, a cone of *gelato* (Italian sherbet) sweetened our return to the island in the hot midday sun.

We cooked over open fires with pots and pans that became black with soot. Soap did not dissolve in seawater, so we had to find a new method of cleaning the pots. We found the answer on the shore. It was not a box of Spic and Span floating on the water but shallow shells from the shore that were filled with calcium deposits. These shells were left by cuttlefish. We scraped the calcium off the shells and cleaned our pots and pans with the powdered calcium.

One day Papá announced that he would like to take a trip along the coast in our folding boats. Hedwig, Werner, and I signed up. Papá and Hedwig manned one boat; Werner captained the second one, with me as his sailor. It would become an unforgettable trip. Our folding boats glided along the coast of the Adriatic, and even though we were aware of the danger of the sharp rocks, which could puncture the canvas, we had no fear. Papá was an excellent sailor and knew the coast of Istria and Dalmatia like his own backyard, or as they say in Austria, "Wie seine Westentasche" (like the pocket of his vest). He knew every island by name and every hidden rock under water along the coast. He was familiar with each bay and even a freshwater stream that issued from the rocks at sea level.

I really learned to know Papá's personality during our trip. He was daring but also cautious when necessary and quietly alert. His directions were specific, drawing upon his knowledge of every part of this area. Werner was just as alert and helpful. We sailed along in perfect harmony, with no fear or anxiety. The deep water was a safe place to be, so we stayed away from the rugged coast. Our first stop was at a freshwater spring. There we filled our containers with ice cold water. As the sun set, we arrived in a bay surrounded by high rocks, which was to be our overnight stopping place.

We pulled the boats onto the land and laid out our sleeping bags. That was no easy task because the shore was covered with stones the

The von Trapp coat of arms.

My paternal grandparents,
August Ritter von Trapp
and Hedwig Wepler,
engagement photo, 1875.

My parents,
Georg and Agathe von Trapp,
after the wedding, 1911.

*My father,
Georg Ritter von Trapp,
in uniform, 1916.*

Kreuzer „Zenta" — Aufnahme während des Einsatzes beim Boxeraufstand in China.
(Aus dem Bildarchiv der Österr. Nationalbibliothek)

The battleship Zenta.

*Tante Connie von Trapp,
Uncle Werner's wife.*

*Our father's brother,
Uncle Werner von Trapp,
circa 1914.*

*Constance von Trapp, our cousin,
known as Connie Baby.*

*My maternal great-grandfather,
Robert Whitehead, inventor of
the torpedo, circa 1900.*

*My maternal grandfather,
John Whitehead (1854–1902).*

*My maternal grandmother, (Gromi)
Agathe Breuner Whitehead, 1911.*

Gromi and her children. Left to right—John, Agathe (my mother), and Frank (top). Mary, Bobby, and Joan (bottom).

Castle Grafenegg, Gromi's childhood home in lower Austria.

Papá in uniform, circa 1935.

*My mother,
Agathe Whitehead von Trapp, 1914.*

Villa Trapp in Pola, the first home of my parents.

*Mamá with Agathe
at the Erlhof, 1913.*

*Mamá with Rupert
and Agathe, 1914.*

*Mamá with Rupert and Agathe
in Fiume, 1914.*

The Erlhof, our home with Gromi during World War I.

Papá and Mamá,
Erlhof, circa 1912.

Gromi, pencil drawing by Tante Joan, 1935.

Mamá knitting in front of the Erlhof, 1915.

Mamá and Papá, Winter 1912.

My first ice-skating lesson with Nenni on Zeller Lake, 1917.

Mamá on skis, Erlhof, circa 1912.

Tante Mary with Rupert and Agathe, Zeller Lake, circa 1915.

Lunch with Nenni holding Maria, circa 1915.

*The four Agathes, 1913. Left to right—Mamá,
Great-Grandmother Agathe Breuner holding Agathe, and Gromi.*

*Agathe and Maria on the occasion of
Great-Grandmother Agathe Breuner's
eighty-fifth birthday, 1918.*

Agathe at age 5, 1918.

Papá and Mamá with Rupert, Werner, Maria, and Agathe, 1916.

Maria, Agathe, and Rupert dressed for Great-Grandmother's eighty-fifth birthday, 1918.

Nenni with Connie Baby, Agathe, Maria, and Rupert (back), Werner and Hedwig (front), 1918.

*Mamá and her children, 1919. Left to right—Hedwig, Agathe,
Mamá holding Baby Johanna, Rupert (back). Werner and Maria (front).*

View from the Hotel Kitzsteinhorn.

The seven von Trapp children in Klosterneuburg, 1922.
Left to right—Rupert, Maria, Agathe, and Werner (back).
Johanna, Martina, and Hedwig (front).

The Martinschlössl in Klosterneuburg,
our home near Vienna from 1921–1925.

Our home in Aigen, near Salzburg, 1925.

We call this photo "The Organ Pipe," circa 1927.
Left to right—Martina, Johanna, Hedwig, Werner,
Maria, Agathe, and Rupert.

Castle Goldegg, the home
of our cousins, the Auerspergs.

Hedwig with her goat in our garden
and Gombo watching, Aigen, 1926.

Agathe, age 18, feeding the chickens with Rosmarie in Aigen, circa 1931.

*Agathe standing next to Gombo with Martina
and Johanna in the cart, Aigen, 1925.*

*The von Trapp family in St. Georgen, Italy,
after leaving Austria, 1938.*

The von Trapp family in Italy, 1938.

Papá in Aigen, 1927.

The von Trapp Family in Merion, Pennsylvania, 1941. Left to right—
Rupert, Agathe, Maria, Johanna, Martina, Hedwig, and Werner (back).
Mother, Johannes, Rosmarie, Papá, and Eleonore (Lorli) (front).

Georg and Maria von Trapp, circa 1943.

Trapp Family Singers rehearsing, 1946. Left to right–Eleonore (Lorli), Agathe, Maria, Papá, Johanna, Martina, Rosmarie, Hedwig, Mother, and Johannes (standing). Werner playing the viola da gamba and Father Wasner on the spinet (seated). Rupert was in medical school.

*Papá playing the violin at
our music camp, circa 1945.*

*Dance music at our summer camp.
Left to right—My sister Maria, a camp guest,
Papá, and Werner, circa 1945.*

Agathe designing linoleum block prints, circa 1941.

World War II ends; Rupert and Werner return safely to Vermont, 1945.

Our new home in Vermont after the blizzard, 1942.

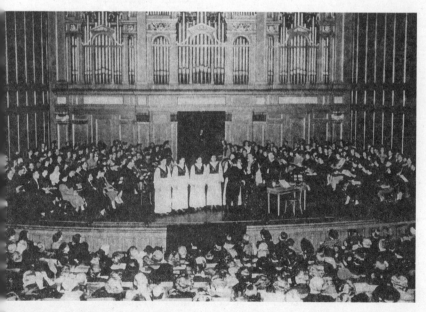

One of several concerts we gave in Jordan Hall, Boston, Massachusetts, mid-1940s.

PEABODY INSTITUTE OF THE CITY OF BALTIMORE
CONSERVATORY OF MUSIC

REGINALD STEWART, Director

EIGHTY-THIRD SEASON OF PEABODY CONCERTS
ONE THOUSAND, ONE HUNDRED AND FIFTY-SEVENTH RECITAL

SIXTH PEABODY RECITAL

SEASON 1948-1949

TRAPP FAMILY SINGERS

First Sopranos
AGATHE VON TRAPP
ELEONORE VON TRAPP

Second Sopranos
MARIA VON TRAPP
MARTINA VON TRAPP

Tenor
DONALD MEISSNER

First Alto
HEDWIG VON TRAPP

Second Alto
MARIA AUGUSTA VON TRAPP

Baritone
WERNER VON TRAPP

Bass
Dr. FRANZ WASNER

Dr. FRANZ WASNER, *Conductor*

FRIDAY AFTERNOON, DECEMBER 17, 1948, AT 3:30 O'CLOCK

CONCERT HALL

JACOB HANDL (1550-1591) — ASCENDO AD PATREM MEUM
The words of this six part motet are taken from the liturgy of the feast of the Ascension of Christ: "I go up to the Father, my Father and your Father, my God and your God. Alleluja. Lifting up his hands, he blessed them and was carried up to Heaven. Alleluja."

WOLFGANG AMADEUS MOZART (1756-1791) — ADORAMUS TE CHRISTE
"We adore Thee, O Christ, and praise Thee, for through Thy holy Cross, Thou hast redeemed the world."

ANTON BRUCKNER (1824-1896) — TOTA PULCHRA ES MARIA
Bruckner, Austrian composer of nine great symphonies, also composed a number of choral works. Among these is this invocation to the Virgin: "All beautiful art Thou, Maria."

TOMÁS LUIS DE VICTORIA (1549-1611) — PASTORES LOQUEBANTUR AD INVICEM
A six part Christmas motet by the great 16th century Spanish composer. "The shepherds said one to another, 'Let us go over to Bethlehem and let us see this word that is come to pass, which the Lord hath showed to us.' And they came with haste and they found Mary and Joseph and the infant lying in the manger."

GEORG PHILIPP TELEMANN (1681-1767) — SONATA in C major. For Alto-Recorder and Virginal
Cantabile; Allegro; Grave; Vivace

HENRY PURCELL (1659-1695) — SUITE from Music to Shakespeare's "Midsummer Night's Dream". For Ensemble
Prelude—Aria—Rondo—Prelude

INTERMISSION—FIVE MINUTES

PETER WARLOCK (1894-1930) — CORPUS CHRISTI
RUTLAND BOUGHTON (1878-) — THE HOLLY AND THE IVY

Carols
Arranged by Dr. Franz Wasner
HIRTEN AUF UM MITTERNACHT (Tyrolian)
CANZONE DI NATALE (Italian)
SHEPHERDS, SHAKE OFF YOUR DROWSY SLEEP (French)

SALZBURG CAROL — THE VIRGIN'S LULLABY
FRANZ GRUBER — SILENT NIGHT

The SEVENTH RECITAL will take place Friday, January 7
TOSSY SPIVAKOVSKY, Violinist

*Program, Peabody Conservatory of Music,
Baltimore, Maryland, December 1948.*

The family on tour in the United States, 1946.
Agathe is on the far right, first row.

Agathe holding a koala bear,
Australia, 1955.

International tour, 1950.

ARTISTS SERVICE OF HONOLULU

(George D. and Dean S. Oakley)

PRESENTS THE

TRAPP FAMILY SINGERS

McKINLEY AUDITORIUM, HONOLULU
MONDAY, MAY 9, 1955

MADAME MARIA AUGUSTA TRAPP, Director
VERY REV. FRANZ WASNER, Conductor

PROGRAM

I.

SING WE AND CHANT IT —(Five Part Ballet)...Thomas Morley
INNSBRUCK ICH MUSS DICH LASSEN..H. Isaac
SWEET HONEY-SUCKING BEES..John Wilbye (1574-1638)

II.

THREE OLD NETHERLAND DANCES..Anon. 16th Century
Recorders
Ronde—Allemande—Pavana (the Battle)
LE ROSSIGNOL EN AMOUR...Couperin
TRIO SONATA IN F MAJOR..Telemann
(Two Alto Recorders, Viola Da Gamba and Virginal)
Affetuoso—Allegro—Adagio—Allegro
PASTORALE...Arr. by F. Wasner
(Recorder, Viola Da Gamba and Virginal—Valentini)

III.

SACRED MUSIC

JESU REDEMPTOR OMNIUM..Gregorian Chant (First Mode)
SALVE REGINA (Six Part Motet)...Orlando di Lassus
SENEX PUERUM PORTABAT...William Byrd
TENEBRAE FACTAE SUNT...Johann Ernst Eberlin
REGINA CAELI, LAETARE...Gregor Aichinger (16th Cent.)

* * *

INTERMISSION

* * *

IV.

GROUP OF AUSTRIAN FOLKSONGS..............................To be Announced from the Stage

V.

FIVE FOLKSONGS..Arr. by F. Wasner
The Oak and the Ash...England
Que lejos ertoy...Mexico
Riguiran ....Spain
Luardo Sertac ....Brazil
Hunting Song ....Germany
HAWAIIAN SONGS..Selected

THE STEINWAY IS THE OFFICIAL PIANO OF ARTISTS SERVICE
Decca and Concert Hall Records

Repertoire Published by G. Schirmer, Inc., New York

Concert program, Honolulu, Hawaii, 1955.

Maria and Rupert,
Vermont, 1991.

BIRTHDAY
CELEBRATION
IN
HONOR
OF
AGATHE VON
TRAPP

Agathe with Werner and Mary Lou at
Agathe's eightieth birthday celebration, March 12, 1993.

Agathe and Mary Lou at their kindergarten in Maryland, late 1980s.

Agathe's eighty-fifth birthday, the Martin Beck Theatre, New York City, March 12, 1998. Left to right—Maria, Johannes, Agathe, and Rosmarie.

Attending The Sound of Music, *New York City, December 1998.*
Left to right—Werner, Maria, Johannes, Agathe, and Rosmarie.

Agathe and Charmian Carr (Liesl
in the movie The Sound of Music),
December 1998.

The von Trapp children in concert,
Foy Hall, Bethlehem, Pennsylvania,
August 2002. Left to right–
Amanda, Sofia, Justin, and Melanie.
Photo by Ryan Hulvat.

The Trapp Family Lodge, Stowe, Vermont.

*Agathe and Maria in front of the family cemetery,
the Trapp Family Lodge, Stowe, Vermont, 2000.*

size of large baking potatoes. We had to move the stones to make a smooth place for our sleeping bags. As we ate the evening meal, a peasant woman in native Croatian dress carried a huge bale of hay on her head as she came down the steep rocks. She walked erect, even when ascending the steep rock on the other side of the beach. She greeted us, and Papá replied with a few words of local dialect.

As we were about to retire for the night, a sailing ship anchored in the bay. To us, it looked like a storybook pirate ship. Papá was worried; I guess he had visions of a confrontation with these strangers. But to his relief, they remained on board, and in the morning, the ship had left.

The next day, the water was calm, and we paddled most of the time. By late afternoon, we reached the next town, the small seaside resort of Lovrano. As we approached the town, I saw a group of young men diving from the steep rocks into the deep water below. Before they dove, they made the sign of the cross. This impressed me deeply. Papá bought provisions, but he wanted to move on since the evening was warm and the sea still calm.

On the beach, we met two German students who offered to tow us out to the deep water. They had an outboard motorboat and were also getting ready to leave. Papá deliberated: *Are these young people trustworthy? Perhaps they are fifth columnists?* (Adolph Hitler had become chancellor of Germany earlier that year. Youthful supporters were often sent in small groups to stir up support for the Nazi Party. They became known as "fifth columnists.") After some hesitation, he accepted their offer, and sure enough in no time at all, we were a half mile out at sea. We waved a "thank you" to them and sailed on.

It was already getting dark, and the island of Kerso stood out as a silhouette against the evening sky. The sea was still calm, the air balmy. Soon the full moon appeared, and the stars came out one by one. We could hear songs coming from fishing boats in the distance as they lit their torches for the night catch. A school of porpoises accompanied us close to our boats on either side. They seemed to enjoy our company. They did not try to overturn our boats or jump over them. Perhaps they thought our boats were some kind of larger dolphin.

The wind freshened. As it did, the canvas that covered our boats started to vibrate. The wind came from behind, and our boats flew over the waves as if we were surf riding. Later in a light breeze, we were able to set sail. We started to sing and moved our boats closer together for better harmonizing. At 2:00 a.m., we arrived at a small island that was owned by a friend of Papá's. It was too early in the morning to make our presence known, so we took our boats on land and slept in our sleeping bags on the pier until the sun awakened us.

Around eight o'clock in the morning, we ventured up the steep path to the house of Papá's friend. At breakfast he told us that the only other inhabitants of the island were a Croatian peasant family who tended sheep, goats, and the orchard. They all seemed to be content living in this splendid isolation away from virtually all civilization.

In the afternoon, he introduced us to the peasant family. They were very friendly and invited us into their home. According to their ancient tradition, these people lived the same life and had the same arrangement in their house as their ancestors had a thousand years before them. The animals lived downstairs, and the family lived above the stable, connected by a primitive staircase. The warmth of the stable rose through the cracks of the floorboards.

The mother of the family showed us their only room, which had beds and some simple pieces of furniture, among them a chest in which she kept their festive attire. She took out the garments of her two daughters for us to admire the intricate embroidery they had done in their spare time. Then she insisted that we try on these clothes. This seemed to be their way of honoring their guests. Of course, Hedwig and I had no choice but to put on these beautiful garments. They consisted of a long black pleated skirt and white linen blouse, embroidered around the wide-open sleeves and around the neck. Over the blouse went a heavily embroidered vest. Every bit of clothing was immaculately clean. The woman took great pleasure in viewing us in her daughters' clothes. Then we returned them to her.

She gave us some special goat cheese called "buina." We took it along to Papá's friend's house. He insisted we try it, telling us how wonderful it tasted. It was sweet and soft with a very fine texture and a somewhat nutty taste. Papá, Werner, and Hedwig had no trouble enjoying this specialty. Only to please our host did I take a tiny piece. Usually I dislike cheese! But I was immediately converted. It really tasted good. I can only compare it to cream cheese, except it had more flavor. Papá's friend also gave us peaches, plums, and grapes from his orchard.

As the day wore on, the wind became stronger, causing white caps to form on the waves. Papá wanted to continue toward Lussin Piccolo, the small island where the widow of a former navy officer, Mrs. Simonić, lived and operated a small pension. But as Papá and his friend watched the waves getting rougher, they decided it would be unsafe for us to continue our trip. Papá's friend invited us to stay on his island until the storm subsided. Papá knew we were being delayed on our adventure, and he wanted to communicate with Mother as to our whereabouts. He sent a telegram back to Pola, thinking it would be delivered to our campsite in Veruda where we had left Mother and the rest of the family.

We spent two days waiting for the wind to calm down, and on the third day, it finally did. We then sailed through another night, arriving early at the pier of Pension Simonić. There we tried to catch a few hours' sleep. Instead, two Italian policemen tried to arrest us as spies! Papá's native dialect and his acquaintance with Mrs. Simonić saved us from an unwelcome delay.

Mrs. Simonić and her daughter, Dori, greeted us like long-lost relatives and gave us a plentiful breakfast. There were other guests at her pension, among them three German students and a young boy who spoke Italian. The three German boys were self-assured, sophisticated, and obviously in sympathy with the Nazi Party.

After dinner, they suggested that the young people take a walk, so Werner, Hedwig, and I went with the Italian boy and the Germans. We ended up at the swimming beach. It was closed for the night, but despite the locked gates, the Germans said, "Let's go swimming!" We pointed out that the gates were locked. "Never mind. We can climb over the fence," they replied. "But we have no bathing suits with us," we objected. "Never mind. It's dark and we'll just go into the water without them." No one said a word until the Italian boy announced, "That is against our religion." I was grateful for that boy's response! With a sigh of relief, the whole group turned and trooped back to the pension.

Before we could start our trip back to Veruda to return to the rest of our family, we had to wait for calm weather. We left from Mrs. Simonić's pension with some of her wonderful whole wheat bread. Papá knew of an island with a lighthouse that lay between Lussin Piccolo and Veruda, and we headed for it. It was too far to sail from Lussin Piccolo to Veruda in one day. We arrived at the lighthouse as a thunderstorm was forming. We just made it to the pier before the first raindrops fell.

The crew from the lighthouse stood on the pier as we arrived. They gesticulated and spoke excitedly in the local Italian dialect. Suddenly one of the men, who had served under Papá's command, recognized him. All of the faces lit up, and the commander of the lighthouse took us in. Only then did Papá reveal the fact that he had an intestinal virus and was in misery. They brought him some medicine and showed us an empty ammunition storage shed where we could spend the night in our sleeping bags.

The next morning one of the crew brought us a huge jug of hot coffee, sugar, a small can of condensed milk, and sea biscuits. It was a wonderful awakening. Papá felt much better by then, and we felt refreshed. The storm raged for two more days. Papá sent a second telegram to Veruda to let the rest of the family know that we were safe but delayed due to stormy weather.

Since we had to wait for better weather, we took a walk around the island. The commander showed us through the tower of the big lighthouse all the way from the bottom to the very top, explaining everything. He also permitted us to look through his telescope, which gave us a full view over the stormy sea. The crew tried to entertain us as well as they could. One member of the crew showed us a tiny seagull standing on his open hand. The men told us that the day we had arrived, they had seen our sails but could not see any boats or people. Their first thought was that we might be spies. They were greatly surprised to see our folding boats, a type of boat they had never seen.

On the third day, a fishing boat was seen coming toward the lighthouse. It was hailed, and when it reached us, Papá asked in Italian if the owner would take us back across the stretch of sea to Veruda. "Yes," he said, "that could be done for a fee." Our boats would not fit on the deck of his boat; however, they could be towed. Papá and Werner manned the folding boats, after tying them to the fishing boat. Hedwig and I were allowed to stay on deck for the voyage back.

Finally Veruda was in sight. But when we arrived, there was no eager waving to greet us or a joyful welcome. When we saw the rest of our family, we could not understand the somber climate that prevailed until Mother said, "Georg, how could you do this to us?"

Papá countered, "But I sent you two telegrams!"

The telegrams were never delivered. The part of our family who had remained behind had been trembling in fear, wondering whether we were dead or alive. Maria later told me that she had prayed fervently for our safety when we did not return on time.

And so our glorious adventure with Papá ended safely. Despite the worries of the rest of the family, the adventure was one of the most beautiful times I can remember with Papá. It was the best introduction to the land he loved. Today Veruda is a fashionable resort with a hotel and a bridge to the mainland, but in our memories, it is still the "Sleeping Beauty" in the sunshine of the Adriatic Sea.

MOZARTEUM // WIENERSAAL

Samstag, 21. August 1937, 20 Uhr

Der
Salzburger
Kammerchor
TRAPP

(Auguste, Agathe, Maria, Hedwig, Johanna, Martina, Rupert und Werner von Trapp)

singt deutsche Volkslieder, deutsche, italienische und englische Madrigale a-cappella

(J. S. Bach, P. Hofhaymer. M. Reger, Orlando di Lasso, Cl. Monteverdi, J. Dowland u. a.)

„ . . Eine Erscheinung, wie sie in der a-cappella-Welt noch nicht dagewesen ist".

Neue Freie Presse, Wien

Karten von S 16.— bis S 2.50, Stehplatz S 1.— an der Tageskasse der Salzburger Festspiele in der Bayernbank, Dollfußplatz 3

11

We Love to Sing

*I*t was a momentous day in 1933 when Mother gathered us together to announce that all our family money was gone. It seems that the bank, which held the funds that Mamá had inherited from her father, had failed, and everyone who had entrusted savings to this bank suffered a loss. Papá took this news very hard. But we children, not realizing the consequences, danced around singing, "Our money is gone! Our money is gone!"

Most of our servants were dismissed because we could no longer pay them. Mother asked us if we could handle the household chores, and, of course, we said yes. We all went to work and enjoyed doing our own cooking and housekeeping. Our butler, Hans, remained with us as well as the laundresses.

Papá owned a parcel of land near Munich, which he sold. Occasionally Papá would give lectures about his life in the navy and his experiences as a submarine commander. So there was some money to help with the living expenses. When our relatives on Mamá's side heard that our money was gone, they sent us a large crate of secondhand clothes! It was well meant, but we had not lost our clothes or our house, only the money in the bank.

Mother had the idea of supplementing our income by renting our rooms; thus, we children were moved to the third floor into the rooms where the maids and the cook had lived. During the summer following the bank failure, two young ladies—one English, the other French—who were cycling through Austria in order to learn German, appeared at our house. They became paying guests and also became our friends.

Another one of our first paying guests was Professor Dillersberger, a priest who taught at the Catholic University of Salzburg. He brought an acquaintance to live with us as well, plus a student of folklore and folk art.

Mother had belonged to the Neuland youth movement during her student days. Some of her happiest experiences were with this group as they wandered from village to village through mountainous regions of Austria. They collected ancient folk songs, wrote them down, and set them to two and three parts for their choir. During summer vacations, Neuland performed on village squares, and once Mother invited the group to sing for us. We were enchanted! They let us have some of their song booklets, and we quickly learned these songs. With all of this new, wonderful music, our family could not stop singing. Anytime a song was appropriate, we sang. No songbooks or music sheets were needed; we sang by heart. Every evening after dinner, we assembled for an hour or two of singing.

It was Professor Dillersberger's responsibility as a priest to say daily Mass before he cycled into town to give his lectures at the university. Mother suggested that we convert our dining room into a chapel and make the music room next door into our dining room. The bishop of Salzburg gave us permission to have a chapel. On Sundays we sang Gregorian chant and other sacred music at Mass. Chorales by Bach were favorites. It so happened that our family had just the right voices to sing four- and five-part music. We had two first sopranos (Johanna and me), two second sopranos (Maria and Martina), two altos (Mother and Hedwig), one tenor (Werner), and one bass (Rupert). Imagine our delight at this discovery!

When Professor Dillersberger had to be away for a little while, he sent in his place a young priest, Dr. Franz Wasner, to say Mass in our chapel. Father Wasner was the assistant director of the seminary in Salzburg. During the Mass, we sang Gregorian chant. Later, at breakfast, Father Wasner made a comment on an error in our rendition and taught us the right way to sing the passage. When Mother discovered that Father Wasner knew about music, she asked him if he could help us with some of the choral singing that we didn't know how to handle.

Father Wasner agreed. He was familiar with the music we wanted to sing, and it was arranged that he come to Aigen on Saturdays to help us. This became a routine. When Father Wasner saw how fast we learned, he introduced us to fifteenth-, sixteenth-, and seventeenth-century music, and researched new music for us in the libraries of Salzburg. From the Neuland group, we had learned some beautiful yodels, folk music, and Christmas carols. All of this made a rich repertoire, which we sang simply for the joy of singing.

The great singer Lotte Lehmann happened to visit us to inquire about renting our house during the Salzburg Festival. Mother asked if we might sing for her, and after she heard us, Lotte Lehmann encouraged us to participate in a yodel competition scheduled for groups of folksingers in Salzburg. We were surprised because our singing was just our personal family hobby, but we entered the competition and won the first prize. I still have this document.

As a result, we were asked to sing a half hour on a radio program. Austria's chancellor, Kurt von Schuschnigg, usually listened to this program. After he heard us, he inquired about the choir from Salzburg and learned that it was the Trapp Family. The chancellor extended an invitation to us to sing at a formal reception he gave for high-ranking officials and their wives in Vienna. Even though Papá did not like the idea of his family singing in public, he agreed, saying that when the chancellor requested us to sing, we could not refuse.

Our family choir—the seven oldest children and Mother, with Father Wasner conducting us—sang our program at the elaborate governmental affair in Vienna in the Belvedere Palace. There were programs by other performers at the same function. After our renditions, the director of the Vienna Choir Boys spoke enthusiastically to Papá, Mother, and Father Wasner. "You must give concerts," he said. There was more discussion about our concert choir, and Mother asked the director what they did in the off-season. He replied that when the Choir Boys were not giving performances, they operated a hotel in the Tyrol. That idea must have impressed Mother and would remain in her memory.

So many people encouraged us to continue singing that a series of concerts was arranged for the 1936–37 season. We sang again twice in Vienna, and while we performed in the small concert hall, the famous American contralto Marian Anderson sang in the large hall in the same building. During the intermission, reviewers wandered over to see what was going on at our concert and what this dirndl-clad singing family was all about. They all seemed delighted with us, and the wonderful reviews in the Vienna newspapers proved it. We were called "das holde Wunder der Familie Trapp" (the lovely miracle of the Trapp Family).

We bought a scrapbook and pasted all the clippings inside. For our second Vienna concert held in the Urania, where I had seen my first movie, Gromi and many of our relatives attended. Gromi was quite surprised and delighted to hear us sing so well as a choir. When we returned to Aigen, we still did not fully understand that we had started a musical career. We simply continued singing because we enjoyed it, and most of our singing was a cappella.

Every summer the Salzburg Festival was a buzzing mecca for performers, agents, and audiences. Concert managers descended upon the city in search of new talent waiting to be discovered. During the 1937 festival, we hired the chamber music hall (Wiener Saal) of the Academy of Music, the Mozarteum. After that concert, impresarios from many countries in Western Europe came swarming backstage to congratulate Papá, Mother, and Father Wasner. Again the message was, "You must give concerts. You have gold in your throats." Our three authority figures realized that they should seriously consider these remarks.

The next day, a lady wearing an alpine hat with a long red feather appeared at our house in Aigen. She introduced herself as a concert manager from France, Madame Octave Homberg, and she engaged us for performances in Paris. Later that day, another manager booked us for concerts in Belgium. Then someone appeared with offers for Holland, Denmark, Sweden, and Norway!

There it was—a whole season of concerts for the Trapp Family Choir for 1937! Among ourselves, we wondered whether we should accept these offers, but it became quite evident that it was meant to be.

Before our concert in the Mozarteum, the director, Professor Bernhard Paumgartner, came to see us. He advised us that we needed an official name for our choir. Until that time, we were giving concerts under any title that the local Austrian managers thought of, such as the Trapp Family Sings, the Trapp Family Choir, and Choir Concert by the Family von Trapp-Salzburg. Now that we were anticipating a concert tour in Europe, Professor Paumgartner suggested we call our group the Salzburg Chamber Choir Trapp. This name was eventually shortened to Chamber Choir Trapp. Later, in America, we were briefly launched as the Salzburg Trapp Choir, soon to be changed to the Trapp Family Choir and finally the Trapp Family Singers.

Professor Paumgartner also suggested that we add instruments to our program. Three of my sisters already played the recorder, having attended a music camp in the Austrian mountains where woodwind instruments were taught. The recorder, an ancient flutelike instrument that is played vertically, experienced a revival in England. Its popularity quickly spread into the German-speaking countries on the Continent.

The professor thought the viola da gamba would be a good addition to the songs of the same period. Papá ordered these instruments from Germany in a set of five. We had planned to add a viola da gamba quintet to our programs, but only Werner, who already played the cello, was able to master its ancient forerunner. The recorders, however, became a charming part of our concerts.

Our tour of Europe was very well received with many standing ovations. In London, December 1937, we were invited to sing at a party held at the Austrian Legation, and Queen Mary was in attendance. It was an honor for us to sing for her, but we did not really get to speak with her. She listened to us, said a few friendly words, and then left.

A freelance agent named Nelly Walter, who had heard us sing in Vienna, urged her friend Charlie Wagner from America to listen to us during the festival. Mr. Wagner, a prominent concert manager in New York City, arrived at our door, asking to hear us sing.

We gave Mr. Wagner a little recital, and when we finished, he asked us if we could sing the Brahms "Lullaby" for him. Of course, we could, and by the time we sang the last note, there were tears in this distinguished man's eyes. He explained that it was a song he remembered from his childhood, and it was one of his favorites. With that, he offered us a contract for fourteen concerts in America, beginning in the fall of 1938 and lasting until early March 1939. We thought of Lotte Lehmann, who had advised us to give concerts in America and how wonderful the audiences were there. "They will love you!" she had predicted.

At first Papá was skeptical about his wife and children singing in public. After all, such conduct was not usual for the family of a high-ranking naval officer. Yet from that time on he faithfully went with us on tour, thus supporting our new life on the stages of the world.

Another series of concerts was added for Italy early in 1938. When we first inquired whether there was a possibility for us to give concerts in that country, we were advised by the Italian consul: "Yes, it is possible, but no one can be sure to get engagements unless the group is a success in Milan and Turin. If they like you in those two cities, all of Italy will be open to you."

Mother liked the idea of touring in Italy because we would have the opportunity to see the great architecture and the artworks of the past in museums and churches. Also the great city of Rome was an attraction because of the ancient ruins and catacombs about which we had learned in our history, Latin, and religion classes.

The audiences of Turin and Milan loved our concerts; as predicted, Italy was open to us. Between concerts, we saw every church, every museum, and every ancient monument. After several concerts, we ended in Rome for a radio program. Father Wasner, who had studied

in Rome, took us on a whirlwind sightseeing tour through the ancient part of the city.

After three days of appreciating churches, monuments, and ancient sites in Rome, Mother suggested we should each return to the one place that impressed us the most. In those days, the public buses were the best way to get around the city. Even though we did not speak Italian, the name of the place we wanted to go was enough to tell the driver where to let us off the bus. We decided to go two by two. That way if we got lost, at least we had each other. However, this arrangement was hardly necessary. The people on the streets of Rome watched out for us! Seeing that a few of us stepped into one bus, they would call our attention to the fact that another part of our group had gotten into a different bus. They did this with excited gesticulations and with loud exclamations in Italian.

How could they tell that we belonged together? Why were they so concerned? We wore our native costumes! All of us girls, plus Mother, were dressed alike in long black skirts with different colored aprons, black jackets, and black hats. The Romans were so used to seeing the different attires of religious congregations, they assumed we were one too. It was as if they thought, *Here comes the Reverend Mother with the sisters.* Someone must have spied the buttons on our jackets, which were embossed with a picture of St. George spearing a dragon, taken from an ancient legend. For that apparent reason, we were named "Sorores di San Georgeo" (Sisters of St. George).

In spite of their efforts to keep us together, each pair found its destination: not the Colosseum, not one of the big churches or the frescoes of the ancient Roman baths, not the Roman Forum, but the great zoo of Rome! As we walked from one animal habitat to another, we met other members of our family. "You are here too? And you too?" All of us had seen enough of the ancient churches and ruins. We were in search of *living things*. The highlight of the zoo was the aviary with a multitude of birds in different sizes, shapes, and colors, chirping away, oblivious to their loss of freedom.

On the way back from Rome, we were booked for a concert in

Assisi, the town where St. Francis lived and founded his order of friars. Our concert was a success. One seventeenth-century madrigal, which imitated the cackling of a hen after she had laid an egg, delighted the young people in the audience. They happily cackled along with us to our great amusement.

After the concert, some family members walked toward the Basilica of Assisi, which was downhill from the house where we stayed. While they were walking, a red spot appeared in the sky above the city of Perugia in the distance. First it seemed as if the city was on fire, but when the brilliant red light spread over half of the vast expanse of the evening sky and moved in the direction of Assisi, it became clear that it was the full-blown aurora borealis (northern lights). I was not along on the walk, but when they told me about what they had just seen, I went outside and stood in awe, taking in the last glimpse of the faint red glow that remained in the darkening sky.

People in the village told us that this was not a regular sunset. It was a sign. In June of 1914, just before World War I started, they had seen the same phenomenon, which they said meant war. It was rare to see such a sight so far south in Europe. When we finished our concert tour of Italy and returned to Salzburg, people there told us that they had seen the same aurora. Little did we know that the beautiful glow we had seen in Assisi was, in fact, a harbinger of what was to come.

~ MARCH ~ 11 ~ 1938 ~

" This is Radio Vienna:
Chancellor Dr. Kurt von Schuschnigg" (is speaking) :

" The German army is at our borders !

I gave orders not to resist because

Austria does not have enough capabilities

to do so. Resisting would only create

a terrible bloodbath! . . . . "

> >

Schubert's Unfinished Symphony
*was interrupted by marches played
with fifes and drums* ....

World War II has begun !

12

The Invasion

T wo months after our concert tour in Italy ended, on the evening of March 11, 1938, the whole family sat listening to music on the radio in Papá's library. At eleven o'clock, the music was interrupted by the announcement that Chancellor Kurt von Schuschnigg was going to speak. We could hardly believe what we heard:

"The German army is at our border with tanks and troops ready to invade Austria." He sounded perfectly calm. "Austria does not have enough capability to avert the German invasion. Resistance would accomplish nothing. It would only cause a terrible bloodbath."

We sat stunned as strains of Schubert's "Unfinished Symphony" followed. For a moment no one said a word. Then the sound of Nazi marches with fifes and drums came through the radio.

The invasion had begun and with it World War II. It was the eve of my twenty-fifth birthday.

Then we heard church bells ringing. The sound was so loud that Papá called the police to find out what was going on. In his mind, there seemed to be no connection between what he had previously heard on the radio and the ringing of church bells. The police gave the answer: "Hitler just marched into Austria."

There it was. But why the ringing of church bells at midnight? That was done only on holy days like Christmas and Easter! The invading German troops had gone into the rectories of the churches and demanded that the bells be rung to welcome them. My birthday was celebrated on March 12 with the usual presents, cake, and candles, but the mood was not festive. We all walked around subdued.

Before lunch on the next day Hans, our butler and handyman, came to talk to Papá. He said that he was a member of the Nazi Party and that we should be careful about what we discussed during meals because he had to report to his superiors everything he heard. Even at that early stage of the war, we could see and feel the changes.

That afternoon several of us bicycled to Salzburg to find out what was going on there. Two bridges for vehicles and two for pedestrians led across the Salzach, the river flowing through the city. We saw German tanks and troops parading from one part of Salzburg across the main bridge to the other side. As we approached the main bridge, we saw that it was festooned with long red Nazi flags with the black crooked cross on a white circle as background. "How did they ever get there overnight?" we wondered.

In those days, when a family member died, the surviving members of that family wore black clothing for a year. After that, they wore black armbands for another year as a sign of mourning. To express our grief over the invasion, I made aprons of black brocade and we wore them over our black native dresses instead of our usual bright colored ones.

Very soon after our trip to Salzburg, Nazi emissaries—actually just teenagers on motorcycles—appeared at our door requesting that we hang the Party flag from our house. Papá told them that we did not have one, but if they wanted to see the house decorated, we could hang a few oriental carpets out the windows! They returned with a large flag, but it never waved from our house. To satisfy the new authorities, the Stieglers, who still lived on the third floor of our house, produced two miniature Nazi flags and hung them from their windows.

After Austria was "liberated," as the Nazis called it, changes were made everywhere in Salzburg. Although merely superficial, one of the changes concerned the traffic. One-way streets became two-way, and vice versa. Other, more distressing changes came about, however; people were vanishing. We heard that the Nazi police force, the black-coated SS men, arrived at homes in the middle of the night and took away one or several of the occupants without explanation of where they were to be taken or when they would be returned. Schoolchildren were interrogated about what their parents discussed at home, who came to see them, and what books they read. Parents became terrified of their own children.

Stories circulated about concentration camps where Jewish people were tortured, starved to death, or gassed and burned in big ovens. Genealogies were investigated, and if any Jewish ancestors were discovered within the last few generations, the family or person was considered Jewish and in danger of being arrested and deported. Fear gripped Salzburg and all of Austria, especially those who were not members of the Nazi Party.

At that time, our family had Italian citizenship. We were citizens of the Austrian city of Trieste, which had become part of Italy after the First World War. Because of this circumstance, all people who were citizens of Trieste automatically became Italian citizens and lost their Austrian citizenship. Ironically, sometime before the *Anschluss* (the Nazi term for the invasion), Rupert had repatriated when he studied at the University of Innsbruck. Mother suggested that the rest of the family also repatriate to Austria. But when Papá looked into this possibility, he found out it was too expensive for the whole family to take this step: it would have cost five hundred Austrian shillings per person. We had lost all our money when the bank failed five years earlier and had just enough to survive by taking paying guests. God was looking out for us! The bank failure had a silver lining; it saved our lives. Since at that time the so-called Axis (the alliance between Germany and Italy) did not yet exist, the Nazis had no legal right to arrest Italian citizens, even if they did not comply with orders or "invitations," as they were called.

After the invasion, Papá received such an "invitation" by letter, ordering him to take command of a German submarine. That, of course, meant he would have to serve in the German Navy. Papá refused. Then our oldest brother, Rupert, who had just finished his medical studies at the University of Innsbruck, was asked to take a position as chief physician in a Viennese hospital. Since all the Jewish doctors had left or had been deported to concentration camps, there was a shortage of doctors. Rupert also refused. Next the Trapp Family was invited to sing over the Munich radio on the occasion of Hitler's birthday. We refused in unison.

The Nazi regime duly noted all these refusals. Had we remained in Austria, we all would have disappeared into a concentration camp as soon as the German-Italian alliance was established.

Sometime after the invasion of Austria, Papá and Mother went to Munich on business. Out of curiosity, they went to see the new museum of art. After viewing some of the exhibits, which had been personally selected by the Führer, they decided to have lunch at the museum restaurant. As they were seated, what did they see? At the table next to them, Hitler and his SS men were also having lunch. Of course, Papá and Mother watched closely to see what transpired. In this situation, they saw Hitler as a private person. He and his followers, when not in the public eye, behaved without restraint, cracking vulgar jokes, laughing loudly and crudely. When our parents came home, they told us about their experience, which we could see left them very troubled now that they had witnessed Hitler's "true face."

Another time when I happened to be in Salzburg with one of my sisters, it was announced that Hitler would make an appearance by motorcade through the town. Everyone expected the Führer to come around the corner any minute. But the minutes became hours. Still no sign of Hitler. Finally after three hours, he appeared riding in his car, standing upright to look over the crowds. He stood very straight so that everyone could get a view of him. He made a speech, as was his usual custom.

A bystander told us that every time his appearance was announced, Hitler came late. He would let the crowds stand lining the streets for hours, waiting for the "great" Führer.

In August, less than six months after the invasion, Hans, our butler, came to talk to Papá and told him that the Austrian borders would soon be closed. No one would be able to leave the country. By warning us, he thereby saved our lives. Hans remained loyal to us even though he was a member of the Nazi Party. We remember Hans with gratitude.

Strangely enough, even before the Nazis came into Austria, I had a strong feeling: if we could only leave this house in Aigen. For no obvious reason, I felt oppressed by the fact that we still lived there, and I hoped we would not have to live in that house much longer.

Even though it was clear to us that we had to leave Austria as soon as possible, given Hans's warning, Mother looked for divine approval concerning the move. Papá called us all together, opened the Bible, and let his finger pick a passage at random. Then he read it to us: "Now the Lord had said unto Abram: Get thee out of thy country, and from thy kindred, and from thy father's house, unto a land that I will show thee" (Gen. 12:1 KJV).

Papá still had to have the consent of each member of his family before accepting and signing the contract from Mr. Wagner for concerts in America. We were sitting around our table when Papá asked each of us, "Do you want to leave Austria and go to America?" Each one said, "Yes, I want to leave."

The first problem to be encountered before we left was that of our clothing. For our tours, we had adopted the native dress of Salzburg in order to solve a very expensive and complicated problem: that of appropriately dressing seven girls at all times. Obviously this problem could not have been solved by civilian clothes, since obtaining fashionable dresses for seven young ladies of different sizes and shapes would have been too time consuming and expensive. The native costumes had to be made before we left the country, so two seamstresses were given the job and did, in fact, achieve the next to impossible.

On the day we left, we had three sets of clothing, two for the concerts and one for traveling. With different colored aprons and white blouses, which we had made at home, our wardrobe was complete. The men wore the traditional suits of Salzburg. In those days, the national dress of the different provinces in Austria had experienced a revival and was fashionable, so we were not conspicuous.

Another problem we faced before leaving the country was what we should do with our house and our furniture. The solution to this problem appeared. Nearby in a suburb of Salzburg called Parsch, the priests of the Boromaeum (a high school for boys who aspire to become priests) were forced out by the Nazis. Their situation came to our attention just at the right time. When Papá offered to rent our house to the displaced priests, they accepted gratefully. After a transaction in which they paid Papá one shilling, they moved into the house.

We found out later that the priests were unable to remain there. The Nazis wanted to rent our house, but Papá told them that we had already rented it to the priests. The Nazis ignored the arrangement, threw out the priests, and took possession. It became Himmler's headquarters during the war. The Nazis built a wall around it, put in extra bathrooms, and built smaller houses on the grounds. At the end of the war, the Americans returned it to us, and we sold it to the Precious Blood Fathers in 1948. We were then able to pay our mortgage in Vermont with this money.

My sister Martina, then age seventeen, wrote a letter to her school friend Erika Klambauer about our last days preparing to leave Austria. Erika graciously gave me permission to translate and incorporate this private letter into my book.

August 23, 1938

Dearest Erika,

The last two weeks we were terribly busy. I did not have time to thank you for your lovely letter. Imagine, just before we left we did get the lire [the Italian currency we needed]. At that same time an acquaintance[1] recommended to us a beautiful small pension not far from Brunico in the Pfuster Valley in North Tyrol, Italy. You know, we were already a little discouraged because we did not know where we should go.

Dr. Wasner did not get a French visa; therefore we could not go to France. Besides, the newest thing is that Italy will not let French citizens into their country, whereupon the French would not let Italians come into their country. There is now no way we can go to France. We are Italian citizens. Too bad, isn't it?!

We wanted to leave from Aigen on Saturday, but in the last minute Papá had such a bad attack of lumbago that he just made it to bed and could not move for a whole week, just at the time when we needed him most.

Shortly before that Lorli came down with appendicitis and was operated on immediately, because we thought it is better to operate now than risk an acute attack on the ship or on any part of the trip. She was very good, unbelievably serious, and quiet. But now she is well again and jumps around as usual and talks as much as ever. Only once in a while when she falls down or walks very fast she says, "My cut [incision] hurts so much."

We had to postpone the transfer of our villa to the Boromaeum for a week. One room after another was cleared out. The furniture was taken partly into the attic and the more valuable pieces were put into one of the upstairs rooms where the Stieglers used to live.

For this final night, five of us girls slept in the room of our former cook, Louise. We slept on iron folding beds. Maria and Johanna slept in the log house in the garden. Werner slept on a bed in the room where the furniture was stored. Only Papá and Mother slept in their own room. [Rupert and Father Wasner had left earlier.]

You cannot imagine what it looked like in our house, and—you know—we had to cook for ourselves and do everything else ourselves because Hans and Louise were not with us anymore. But Frau Mareck and Frau Hlavka still helped out. [They did our laundry.]

We cleaned up the whole house, prepared it, and did all that one does when one rents one's house.

Then we packed our suitcases, and on Friday, we turned our house over to the priests.

We ate lunch at the local restaurant Flachner. In the evening we had finished just about everything.

Do you know what we did after that? We went to Maria Plain[2] in Blecher's and Gruenbart's Taxis.[3]

The night was balmy and the sky clear, covered with stars. It was wonderful. The church was already locked, but the caretaker unlocked it for us and lit all the candles on the altar. There we received our last blessing in Austria.

Maria Plain is really beautiful, especially at night. Then we had something to eat in the restaurant and sang a little while in the meadow near the small shrines, just to say GOOD BYE!

Saturday morning at six o'clock we had Mass. After that, there were the last tasks to be done, and we cleared the rooms we had slept in. At last we took our suitcases to the train station.

At 9:30 a.m. the train left, and this was an indescribable feeling.

We were totally exhausted after all this work. We never got to bed before 10:30 p.m. or midnight and got up at 6:00 or 6:30 in the morning. Then running up and down between attic and cellar and bicycling back and forth between Salzburg and Aigen—that is nothing to laugh at.

Besides you must not forget, and this is the worst: Your "Uncle" Forstner[4] came on Friday to look at his room. It was going to be the room in the middle, a very big room where Maria and Agathe used to sleep and where the linden tree stands in the room. He obviously did not like it because that is how he acted. He announced, "I do not care, it's all the same. So, now I just have to move into this house. If the big wardrobe [an antique] cannot be taken out, I just have to leave my own at home." A home he did not have anymore because the Nazis took it over. He continued: "And the tree; it has to go. I have no use for it."

You know, I think this is very strange, but men are always terribly awkward and impractical. I don't understand why he did not like the linden tree, and the rooms are certainly better than those in the Boromaeum are, especially his because I know it. One should not cling so much to earthly things, don't you think?

I have never seen him in such a bad frame of mind, but at that time he was in a very bad mood, or—how should I say it?

Do you know what else I did? I bought myself a pair of straw slippers, just like the ones you have. My sisters and brothers liked them too. Anyway now we start becoming elegant. Too bad I cannot show you the beautiful handbag and the lovely aprons and the long-sleeved Sunday dirndl. I thank you in the name of the whole family for lending us your pattern. It was really a great success.

Here we are now, sitting in a very clean and cozy country restaurant in St. Georgen, Italy. Around it are meadows, mountains, and alpine pastures strewn with large rocks. Horses and geese are grazing freely in the village.

The pastor is terribly nice and entrusted us with a second key to the church, as well as with one for the shrine close by. We can say our evening prayers there. Isn't that wonderful?

This coming Sunday we shall sing the High Mass in the church of St. Georgen. I am looking forward to that. You know we have Mass every morning at 7:30. After breakfast we practice singing. At 11:00 those of us who play the recorders practice until lunch. After lunch each one of us can do what we want until 5:00 p.m. From then on we sing until supper.

The border officials would not let our spinet [a small, ancient keyboard instrument] cross the border. Not even when we said we are only traveling through Italy. That is why Papá went back to the Brenner Pass [a mountain pass between Austria and Italy] to clear that up with the officials.

In spite of the fact that it rained until yesterday, it is very beautiful here. If you could only be here! I am really surprised that you had not climbed the Gaisberg [a mountain] again since our last excursion.

Today there was a chimney fire in a house almost adjacent to the inn where we are staying. Fortunately, the chimney sweep happened to be in the restaurant and readily knew what had to be done. However, it did look awfully dangerous. The iron doors of the chimney were already red hot and on top of it all, the house has a wood shingle roof insulated with straw underneath. That was a real shock.

Your kind parents invited me to come to Seeham for one or two days, but really I cannot stay away from home now. I have to write somehow from here and hope the letter arrives because I addressed it "Seeham, Poste Restante."

I feel sorry for you that you have to learn French and that the coffee and the melons taste so bad. Here we have very good fruit. You already have quite a French handwriting.

Dear Erika, I cannot keep writing or else I will make more mistakes. I do hope you are not mad at me for not having written to you for such a long time.

Love,
Martina

P.S. Werner and Rupert send you greetings.

As Martina mentioned in her letter, this is how we left our house in Aigen:

The day after we gave the house to the priests of the Boromaeum we had Mass at 6:00 a.m. After breakfast we completed our last-minute tasks, then we quietly walked out of our door, not knowing whether we would ever come back.

Each one of us carried a rucksack (knapsack) on his or her back and a large suitcase in one hand. We took only what we could carry. We did not climb over a mountain; we just crossed the railroad tracks behind our property, proceeded to the station, Aigen bei Salzburg, and took the first train south to northern Italy. We stayed there in a small pension, as Martina reported to her friend Erika, until the day came that we had to leave the friendly village and the beautiful countryside of St. Georgen. Because the Italian government would not send Papá's navy pension out of the country as long as he resided in Austria, he was able to collect a lot of back pay when we went to St. Georgen. It was enough to sustain us through the summer and get us to London. We had our passports, our visas, a contract, and passage to the United States of America in our possession. In March 1939, our visas would expire.

We boarded the train to France through Switzerland, had a rather choppy crossing through the English Channel, and then did a few hours of sightseeing in London.

On Friday, October 7, 1938, at 3:00 p.m., we boarded the train to Southampton where the *American Farmer* was docked. She left the

harbor at 6:00 p.m. with seventy-five passengers on board. I remember seeing the rocky coast of Land's End as we passed the English landmark in the evening light. It was very impressive. The thought ran through my mind: *We are leaving Europe and our old life behind!*

13

We Come to America

Early one morning in mid-October 1938, the skyline of New York came into view. No one on board the *American Farmer* wanted to miss the exciting moment when we entered New York harbor. The passengers were lined up on deck to get the first glimpse of the New World. A rosy mist lingered over the city, but outlines of the buildings were easily distinguishable. For the first time, we saw the skyscrapers about which we had heard so much. It was an unforgettable moment when, after ten days at sea, we saw America.

Slowly the ship moved toward the pier. With great anticipation, we waited until it was time to leave the ship that had become a home for us as well as for the kind passengers and crew who had made the days at sea not only bearable, but also a wonderful experience.

Someone from the office of Charlie Wagner, our New York agent, met us at the pier and made sure that all of us, plus our mountain of luggage, arrived safely at the Hotel Wellington. Anyone who happened to be in the vicinity that day would have seen quite a spectacle. There were ten adults in strange clothing with two little girls, ages seven and nine. Each person had a large suitcase and a rucksack. There were three large suitcases for the concert attire, a case containing the spinet, a different case for the four legs of the spinet, five violas da gamba, one suitcase for the recorders, and one

suitcase for the expected baby. It was difficult to believe how much luggage one family could have. Even though the amount of luggage might have been a shock for the doorman, somehow it all disappeared into the hotel and ended up in the right rooms.

Before we went to bed that first night in the hotel, we put our shoes outside our rooms so that they could be shined, as was the custom in Europe. We had worn the same shoes during our long journey from Italy to New York. At midnight the night watchman knocked on our doors and shouted, "Take your shoes into your rooms or tomorrow morning they might not be there anymore!" "Aha," we realized, "in American hotels you must shine your own shoes." It was our first lesson on American soil.

The Wellington became our home for a week until the concert tour started. Therefore, we had that amount of time to learn our way around and to find the sights and places we wanted to visit. Since Papá, Mother, and Father Wasner dealt with our manager about all major matters, our responsibilities included knowing our music, especially important for those of us who played the recorders, keeping our clothes clean and tidy, and being on time for rehearsals. Because Father Wasner was in charge of payments, we had to be together for the meals, which were also times when everyone could be accounted for.

The Hotel Wellington was one of the places in New York City where many artists from overseas were "parked" until they had their concert schedules, transportation, and day of departure. From our rooms, we could hear the musicians practice their instruments. Sometimes the music that we heard throughout the hotel sounded like a small orchestra tuning its instruments: here a violin, there a trumpet, from another apartment the sound of an oboe, and a clarinet floating up the shaft of the courtyard. Occasionally the voice of a singer could be heard, which added yet another dimension.

An Ursuline convent in Brooklyn, run by very kind sisters, was recommended to Mother as a school for the two youngest girls, Rosmarie and Lorli, to board while we went on tour. Although they were not happy with the arrangement, we knew of no other place where we could leave them. There they would be safe and could not escape into a world unknown to them. They could learn English and other subjects until we could take them along with us again.

On the morning of our first concert, Charlie Wagner handed us our schedule and announced that we would travel in a chartered bus. The driver's name was Mr. Tallerie. We were assured that Mr. Tallerie would get us safely from city to city and from concert hall to concert hall. He was experienced in driving groups like ours, and he would be able to answer our questions.

Mr. Tallerie, who was to be our driver for two years, was all that Mr. Wagner had told us and more. I will never forget him as our first friend in these United States. A perfect gentleman, of French descent, always polite and courteous, he seemed to be aware of his responsibilities, not only as our driver, but also as our teacher about everything in America. I think he felt obligated to educate newcomers to the United States who came with European ideas, which did not always fit into the American landscape. He did a very good job. He was helpful in other ways as well, such as loading and unloading our baggage, and he drove the bus with élan. His favorite expression was, "Let me tell you something."

Our bus, painted a royal blue, was specially outfitted. It had a total of thirty-two upholstered seats, grouped in twos, in rows along either side of the bus. There was another upholstered seat across the back of the bus. A metal cot was placed alongside the last two windows to the left in case someone needed to lie down. Even with all these choices, the window seats were the favorites. On the outside of the bus, on both sides and above the front window, was the announcement "Trapp Family Choir." It was quite impressive for us to see our name officially displayed on the vehicle in which we were to live and ride during the following weeks.

Our first concert was scheduled in Easton, Pennsylvania. Traveling there gave us our first experience with American highways. We found it remarkable that the traffic was so well organized and that the roads were paved. What a difference from what we were used to! There were no paved roads in Austria at that time. Some stretches were covered with gravel. Virtually all of the roads had potholes in which the rainwater collected, and one could not see how deep the holes were, which made the roads very dangerous.

People in the United States seemed so nonchalant about this wonderful blessing of paved highways marked with a middle line of white paint—and stoplights regulating the traffic. In Austria a driver was at the mercy of the other motorists. Ah, gas stations, what a blessing! They were not only for refueling but also for other necessities. We were very excited that we could get a drink there and a free map of any state. For Mr. Tallerie none of this was new, but for us it was all new and wonderful.

Whenever we traveled in the evening, I was intrigued by the rows of red brake lights in front of us and the white lights coming toward us on the opposite lane. I wondered how a Roman soldier of ancient times would feel if he could come back and see these seemingly endless rows of lights on our highways. Would not that sight give him the shivers? To us in the twenty-first century, this sight is an everyday occurrence taken for granted; yet I have never stopped being in awe of the traffic at night on the highways of the United States of America.

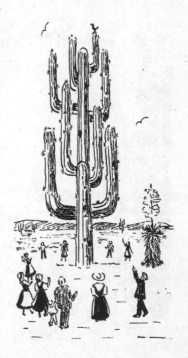

Mother always managed to see something interesting to photograph, asking Mr. Tallerie to stop "right then and there." He would then come out with his favorite line— "Mrs. Trapp, let me tell you something: I cannot stop here!"—after which he gave her a lecture of what he could or could not do while driving sixty miles per hour.

Sometimes we saw sights that we had not seen anywhere in Europe. As we were traveling across the United States, we noticed boxes on posts all along the road and questioned Mr. Tallerie. He said, "These are mailboxes. The mailman rides along the highway, stops at the box, and puts the mail in. Handy, isn't it?"

On the way to California, we were riding through the desert—the land of the famous giant cactus. We had never seen or even heard of this phenomenal plant. When Mother spotted an especially well-preserved giant, she asked Mr. Tallerie to stop the bus. She wanted to take a picture. Of course, we all wanted to look at the unusual sight. It felt as if we were transported back in time to the era of the dinosaurs. We noticed many little holes in those huge branches where the birds had made their nests. The whole area before us was filled with cactus birdhouses.

Whenever there was time, Mr. Tallerie would drive us to a place of interest, especially when our route went past the site anyway. For

instance, the Natural Bridge, one of the wonders of the world, was located on the way to our concert in Virginia. Even Mr. Tallerie agreed we must see that. After parking, we walked down into the gorge that the river had formed over thousands of years. At the bottom of the gorge, we found seats prepared for tourists from where we could hear an "invisible" organ playing soft music like "Carry Me Back to Old Virginny," "My Old Kentucky Home," and other favorites. Above we could see the miraculous arch of the Natural Bridge and the traffic on the highway moving right over it.

As we traveled farther south, we rode through cypress swamps. There, large trees with oversized trunk roots grew right out of the water, and long strands of Spanish moss hung from their branches. Once when the bus stopped for a lunch break along one of these pondlike areas, Papá and Werner could not pass up the

opportunity to take a boat ride. An old rowboat was sitting at the water's edge, just "asking" for someone to take it out into the cypress pond. Surprisingly an oar had been left in it. If Papá could not have the sea, even a pond in which cypress trees grew would satisfy the deep longing for what was now only a memory for him. A seafaring captain will always yearn for the sea.

We continued on the long highway passing through Alabama, Mississippi, and Louisiana. In one of these states, we saw the strangest thing. Along the right and left sides of the highway were signs spaced so that the motorists could plainly read them while driving. One of these sentences read, "The Flowers Bloom, the Grass Is Riz, Where Last Year's Drunken Driver Is! BURMA SHAVE."

To our great consternation another message that was spread out along the highway read "Jesus Saves." We could not understand how anyone could put these holy words, which belonged in a church, on the side of the road. Again Mr. Tallerie had the answer. "Here in the South," he said, "the Christians believe in sharing their belief with the unsuspecting motorists. They feel that the message gives the motorists something to think about. Also, this is a free country, and anyone can say anything he wants, where he wants, and when he wants."

Another shock was an oversized milk bottle standing next to the highway. Mr. Tallerie had to stop the bus and drive back so that Mother could take a picture of it. What a novelty! While Mother took the photograph, I took my sketchbook to eternalize in pen and ink this, to me, horrendous and unsightly object. It was not only the size of the giant milk bottle that impressed us but also the audacity of whomever placed it there. Imagine ruining the beautiful landscape with such an atrocious object. Above the bottle was advertised "Cream When You Want It—Ohio Cloverdale Golden Jersey Milk—Helps Toledo Grow!" Even though we saw other things that disturbed us along the highway—such as dead trees, which were not cut down, large pieces of dead wood along the highway, and unharvested apples—nothing could top the giant milk bottle.

As for the dead wood, I thought, *What is the matter with the American people that they do not take care of these things?* In Austria the poor grandmothers have the official privilege of collecting the dead wood in the forest. They take away every little branch and twig, bundle them, and take them home for firewood in the winter, or they sell them for kindling. Why do the people in America waste all that good firewood and the ripe fruit?

Again Mr. Tallerie had the answer to this problem of what seemed to us incomprehensible waste: "Let me tell you something. This is a vast continent. There are not enough people to clean up the landscape. Who wants all that dead wood anyway or these sour apples under the trees? Besides, the things that are lying around are not worth the money it would cost to take them away."

Another lesson learned! This is not Austria; this is another continent. This is America, and here we do things differently! Mr. Tallerie was a good sport and always obliged if possible. I think he liked us; we remember him with affection.

Our first concert tour was the most difficult one. A typical program in December 1938 might have included the following numbers, among others: "Trio Sonata for Two Recorders in F and Figured Bass" by Telemann; "Fantasy in C" by Handel; "Es ist ein Ros entsprungen" by Praetorius; and "Ave Maria" by Mozart. Even though we knew our music practically in our sleep, we were still apprehensive about whether or not the American audiences would like our concerts. But the audiences were very attentive. From the moment we began to sing, peace descended on the audience. In one rural town, however, the peace wasn't even broken by applause. We thought they didn't like our music until the local manager explained, "They don't know how to act at a concert."

Mother was expecting a baby, which was to remain a secret. Every day we worried that the baby might appear too soon. The shaking of the bus or the roar of the locomotive on the tracks that passed by our hotel at night was enough to send shivers through the whole family. Did Mother get safely through the night? We were also concerned about potholes or big stones on a stretch of road under construction. We still worried, even though the whole family prayed fervently for God to protect Mother and our new baby.

Around Christmastime, Charlie Wagner discovered, to his dismay, that there was a baby on the way. He canceled the remaining concerts. We had no more income, no place to stay, and almost three more months in the United States before our visas expired.

In this predicament, Professor Otto Albrecht, a music lover who had heard our concert at the Museum of Art in Philadelphia, came to our rescue. He looked for and found a small house in Germantown, Pennsylvania, that we could rent. There, in the middle of January 1939, to our great joy and relief, Johannes was born.

Mother had promised God that if the baby was born healthy and with all its faculties intact, she would take him or her in thanksgiving to the shrine near St. Georgen in Italy where we had been awaiting our first passage to America. Now she would fulfill her promise.

When our visas expired on March 4, 1939, we boarded the French liner *Normandie*. It was the most luxurious and elegant ship imaginable, the only one leaving for Europe on March 4 that had enough space for our large family in tourist class. It was so large that we could get lost trying to find our cabins. We were given a pass, which allowed us to walk all over the huge liner. Also, the captain arranged for us to give a gala concert during the voyage.

1939

Our first concert was scheduled for March 12 in Copenhagen, Denmark. We didn't have much time to get there, but we made it. We spent that spring giving concerts in the Scandinavian countries. The people there were very friendly and helpful. I still remember one elderly grandmother in Copenhagen who saw us carrying baby Johannes around and insisted on lending us a lovely baby carriage.

In June we moved on to Holland. There, the president of KLM airlines, Mr. Menton, and his wife had invited us to stay in their guest house adjoining their beautiful home and had arranged a private concert for their friends and acquaintances. After several days, he moved us to a sweet little cottage in the dunes, which was their summer home. During these wonderful weeks, we shared our household duties, practiced our concert repertoire, and otherwise were free to do anything we wanted. I made some sketches of family members doing their chores as well as some of the dune landscapes.

Since refugees were allowed to stay only a certain number of weeks in one of the unoccupied countries, we had to move on in July, and we split up. Father Wasner and Rupert did not go back to Austria but waited in a French town in Alsace-Lorraine. Papá and Mother, with baby Johannes, went back to St. Georgen, Italy, in order to give thanks in the little shrine on the hill behind the inn where we had stayed the summer before. Werner and the girls went back to Austria to stay with relatives; two of Mamá's cousins took us in.

Because no concerts were scheduled during July, I decided to take a bicycle trip to visit some other relatives of Mamá's in their summerhouse by a mountain lake. I had heard about the beauty of this place and wanted to see it. Along the way I could draw sketches of the countryside, the way I had done in Scandinavia. The scenery exceeded my expectations; I filled many pages of my sketchbook, and I still have these sketches. When it got dark on the first day, I stopped at a country inn for the night. I noticed that I needed a clean set of sheets and, overcoming my shyness, asked for clean sheets, which were given to me along with a lame apology.

The next day I started out again on my bicycle, and in the middle of nowhere, I had a flat tire. As I was pushing my bicycle up a hill, wondering if I would have to walk the rest of the way, an old farmer on a bicycle stopped to ask if he could help. I replied, "Yes, I have a flat tire. Could you tell me where I could have it fixed?" He said that he had something with him to repair tires. It did not take him long, and my tire was as good as new. I thanked him and was about to continue on my way when he invited me to stay overnight in his house. I declined politely and told him that I wanted to reach my relatives before dark.

When I finally arrived at their home, I was greeted by two elderly ladies who were surprised to see me. They were not the relatives that I remembered, so I introduced myself and they invited me in but were not very friendly. They seemed to be reluctant to share their food with me, especially the butter. The next morning they put me to work taking care of their two grandchildren. I could sense that I had come uninvited and at the wrong time. It never occurred to me to write to them in advance to ask if a visit was convenient! We had always lived as a family group, and our authority figures made all the arrangements for us. It had never fallen on me to be involved with the preparations. I just thought my relatives would be happy to see me. How could they if they did not even know who I was?

Since I did not feel welcome there, I decided to leave the next day, but I did take time to sketch the house that was situated at the base of a steep rock. Two little peasant boys came along to see what I was doing and asked me to draw their pictures. I was glad to comply, and the boys were delighted with their likenesses. On the way back, I filled another sketchbook. In spite of the attitude I encountered from the two ladies, I remember it as a very enjoyable adventure. Thirty-five years later I converted some of the sketches from this trip into watercolors and exhibited them in a gallery in Reisterstown, Maryland.

At the end of July, the whole family was to meet in Amsterdam, Holland; by the grace of God, we did. Our former manager in Sweden had arranged more concerts there as well as a place for us to stay on one of the small islands in the southern part of Sweden. We lived in little cabins on a former farm with a central house as a dining room

MERAMHAUS IM GRUNDLSEE

for the guests. In that climate, all the fruit trees were laden with ripe fruit. There on the old trees grew cherries, apples, and pears. Also growing were strawberries, cranberries, and blueberries—all ripe at the same time and could be had for the picking.

It turned out to be one of the most enjoyable summers we ever spent. Somehow Papá was able to have our two folding boats, which we had on the island of Veruda, shipped to this island. We made little excursions with them on the lake, but we had to be back in time for rehearsals. Papá also hired bicycles for us so we could ride through the island and discover all the interesting relics, which remained untouched, from ancient Viking times. There again I had time to make sketches.

In the main house, we heard international news being broadcast on the radio. One day we heard the shocking news that Hitler had directed his blitzkrieg into Poland. From then on, at least one member of our family was always listening. Hedwig actually kept a diary of these newscasts. After that our Swedish manager got nervous that he might have to join the army, so he canceled several of the concerts he had arranged. Our last concert was held in Karlskruna, Norway, after which we were to cross the ocean again for a second tour in the United States under the management of Charlie Wagner.

In all of the European countries where we gave concerts, our performances were two hours long with one intermission. We sang serious sacred music, sixteenth- and seventeenth-century madrigals in English, Italian, and German in the first part of the program; folk songs made up the second part. The response from the audiences was overwhelming—standing ovations and people streaming backstage after the concerts to tell us how much they loved the performance. The reviews were written by people who understood music, and what they wrote was beyond our expectations. They praised our performances in even the smallest details. Now, after more than sixty years, I am overwhelmed by the high praise given to us by the music critics who wrote for the newspapers. These reviews were excellent, without exception, in every country: Austria, France, Belgium, Sweden, and Norway.

After one of our concerts in a small town in a thirteenth-century Swedish church, the pastor came out of the church as we were leaving to embrace Father Wasner. He thanked him, in tears, for the wonderful music he had just heard.

From Oslo we left on the *Bergensfjord*, a troop ship that had been transformed for passengers and was the last ship that left Norway to take refugees to the United States. Since Charlie Wagner was late in getting our tickets, we were fortunate to be assigned the last available cabins, located on the lowest deck of the ship. This meant a smoother voyage since the lower deck rolled the least. There were just enough cabins for our family as well as one for Father Wasner and one for Martha, a former classmate of Maria, who would take care of Johannes, the baby.

When we arrived in New York harbor on October 7, 1939, after an uneventful crossing, one of the customs officials became suspicious of a harmless remark that Mother made to him about wanting to stay in the United States forever. Rupert was allowed to leave the ship because he had acquired an immigration visa. The rest of us, however, had only six-month visitors' visas, and we were taken to Ellis Island. At that time it was still a large detention facility for foreigners in the harbor of New York. The customs officials boarded ships arriving from overseas, detained any suspicious person or group of people, and took them to Ellis Island. Documents were scrutinized and personalities assessed. A doctor was on hand to separate the healthy from the sick and to detect any contagious diseases. These officials had a grave responsibility, which they took seriously. Having dealt with criminals and swindlers, they had an attitude toward newcomers that was stern, strict, and professional. They fired a list of direct and unexpected questions at the newcomers. If people did not answer to their satisfaction, they had the authority to take these individuals into custody.

When Mother indicated that she would like to stay forever in America, our whole family became suspect in the eyes of the customs authorities. So, while they checked on our credentials, we were detained for several days on Ellis Island. It was quite an experience for us who had never seen a detention camp from the inside.

We were led into a narrow corridor, which looked like it needed a good cleaning and a coat of paint. In fact, the facility in general needed remodeling. The whole place was dismal. The faces of the officials and wardens were taciturn, and we could not detect even a hidden smile or the smallest sign of compassion. Everything was done in a cold and serious manner. Any conversation was strictly to the point. At a special hearing, Mother answered all their questions truthfully, but at the end of a two-hour inquisition, the official told her, "We don't believe you."

After signing in, we were led into the big hall where all the detainees had to spend their daytime hours. There were several groups of people huddled together. Some were just sitting on the floor, some on the benches doing nothing. Near us we saw a group of Oriental people, obviously a family, who combed each other's hair and looked for lice. No one talked. We were not permitted to talk to our "fellow prisoners" about our case, but we did entertain them with our music.

The dining hall was large with long tables arranged in rows. The room looked like a waiting room of a train station at the beginning of the twentieth century. The walls were empty of any art to lift the spirits. The food was served on large tin plates. Possibly those plates had seen the faces of the first immigrants.

Our table was next to a table occupied by a group of young Chinese boys. They had already spent two years on Ellis Island, not being allowed to enter the United States. They filed into the dining room as fast as they could, sat down, took the salt and pepper shakers, and showered their portion of rice with the only spice available to enhance their daily rations. They did not look downcast, but they were obviously very hungry.

After lunch we were allowed to go out into the yard for a half hour. A warden accompanied and counted us, going out and coming in. Even though we were restricted to certain areas, there were no cells or bars, as in a real prison. We were allowed to walk freely without handcuffs.

The dormitories for men and for women were upstairs. The lights were left on all night, and a warden checked several times at night to see if every person was in bed. Papá, Father Wasner, and Werner had to sleep in the men's dormitory. Mother, the baby, and we girls were assigned a dormitory together. No other person was with us. Mother asked if we could have permission to sleep with the lights turned off. Because of the baby, the request was granted by the authorities. Having the lights off was a great relief. We were sorry for Papá, Father Wasner, and Werner, however, who could not enjoy this comfort.

Rupert worked tirelessly to get help to free us. After three and a half days of not knowing if we would be sent back to Southampton, our entire group was released through the help of kind American friends we had met the year before, who vouched for us. The occasion was joyful! Even those refugees left behind joined together to cheer and applaud selflessly. Although our days on Ellis Island were very humiliating, especially for Mother who had caused our detention, we received great publicity by being detained there. Our manager did not mind that a bit!

At the end of our second tour, Hitler's blitzkrieg in Europe was already in full swing. One country after another fell under Hitler's steamroller, and refugees from those countries had permission to remain in the United States. After our last concert tour with Charlie Wagner, we were fortunate to be accepted by Columbia Concerts under the management of Freddy Schang.

A wonderful surprise awaited us one day after our return from this tour. Mr. and Mrs. Drinker, who owned a beautiful estate in Merion, Pennsylvania, and who had heard us sing, offered us a temporary home across the street from their home. They knew that we had no place to stay in the off-season, and when Mr. Drinker's mother, who had lived in the house, died during this concert tour, they thought of us.

Mr. Drinker was an attorney and a music lover who directed his own choir of music lovers. He added a small concert hall to his house in order to accommodate his singers. There they gathered for evenings of music making of the highest quality. With great enthusiasm Mr. Drinker conducted chorales and cantatas by Johann Sebastian Bach and other composers of that period. He was so fascinated with Bach's music that he decided to translate all of Bach's cantatas into English.

Since he did not speak German, Mr. Drinker must have used a dictionary for his translations, which would have been rather difficult and slow going. Out of nowhere, so to speak, came a group of people who sang Bach's music and whose conductor could speak both languages—and these people had no place to stay.

Mr. Drinker proposed a deal to us: we could live free of charge in the now vacant house he owned if Father Wasner would help him with the translation during our off-season, and if we would come over occasionally to sing for his choir. At that point, two musicians found each other, and our family did not have to worry about where we would live. Coincidence? Hardly!

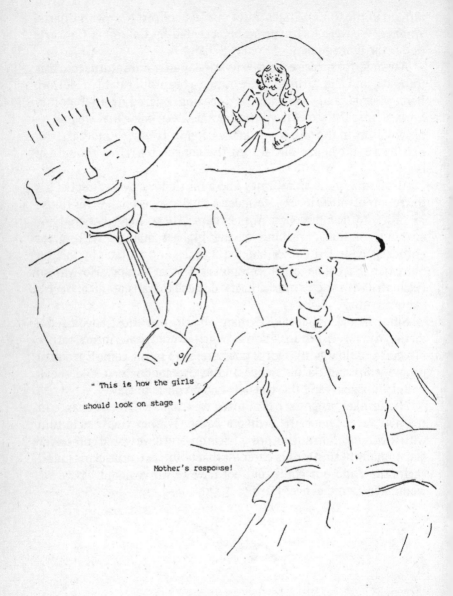

14

On the Road as the Trapp Family Singers

In 1940, Columbia Concerts, Inc., of New York took over the job of managing our singing tours. Freddy Schang became our personal manager; he guided and shepherded us for the next sixteen years. After our audition, Freddy had numerous suggestions. First, he said we needed to change our name from Trapp Choir to Trapp Family Singers. He thought that the new name would have more audience appeal and would better characterize us as a family, not just a group of singers. We agreed enthusiastically to the change. *Choir* was too limited and sounded too serious.

His next suggestion did not fare so well. Freddy had the audacity to suggest that we, the ladies in the family, wear high-heeled shoes on stage! We all protested, and Mother was emphatic on the matter. "Our children were not brought up to wear high heels, and they cannot walk in them. What we wear is part of our native dress. Also, high heels are bad for the feet!" were her arguments. Freddy gave in. We were allowed to wear our own shoes on stage.

Freddy's next request concerned our appearance on stage. Our dresses were fine, but our faces were too pale. Freddy convinced us that we needed to put on makeup, so we used a minimal amount before we went on stage. He had no complaints about the attire of the men in our group.

In our minds, his last request was the strangest of all. He wanted us to smile on stage! *How absurd*, we thought. We had given concerts all over Western Europe without cracking a smile on stage— concerts in prestigious concert halls that lasted two hours. We had received standing ovations in France, Belgium, Italy, and the Scandinavian countries without smiling.

Freddy had even more to say. He thought our concerts were too long and too serious, and they lacked contact with the audience. He told us that American audiences want "light, happy music."

It was up to us to adjust to Freddy's requests. Father Wasner went to the Music Library in New York to find "lighter, happier music" for our concerts. I am glad that Freddy did not find out that we knew many Austrian folk dances. He might have asked us to dance on stage too.

After all these changes had been made to Freddy's satisfaction, and we promised to try to smile, he booked us as the Trapp Family Singers for a tour of 107 concerts over an eight-month period. Again we got into the blue bus with our new name written on it. Under our new management, Rudi was our driver.

The concert season ran from October to Christmas and from January until after Easter. Freddy Schang booked us from coast to coast with local groups, known as Community Concerts Associations, and we gave concerts all across the United States and Canada. We performed in the grandest concert halls of large cities: Jordan Hall, Boston; Orchestra Hall, Chicago; Masonic Auditorium, Detroit; and Town Hall, New York City, to name a few. We also sang in smaller cities where the people were hungry for music. For those concerts, we performed in high school auditoriums, movie theaters, churches, and colleges. In Washington, D.C., we sang in an outdoor amphitheater to thousands of people.

From the beginning, American audiences were appreciative of our concerts, congratulating us in letters or after the performances. In towns and cities, small and large, the critics gave us the most generous reviews. The following excerpts were taken from a mid-1940s souvenir booklet that did not give dates or names of publications:

One can scarcely imagine singing more touching than that of the Trapps. They are harmonious, very quiet, straightforward, and wholly united. They don't go in for theatrical pathos or vocal effect. They sing the music and the words as sincerely as they might recite the Lord's Prayer.

New York City, New York

A performance by the Trapps is a unique experience. It is an adventure in music mingled with an adventure in personalities. It begins with music and musicianship of the first order of integrity. Then there is the great appeal of the musicians themselves.

Toledo, Ohio

The beauty of the music recreated by the pure flute-like voices carried one far from the passions and sorrows of the world. It seemed that Fra Angelico angels had come to life.

Louisville, Kentucky

When the Family had completed singing, so taken aback was the audience that a full 30 seconds elapsed before it broke into applause . . . . Then the hall was filled with thunderous acclaim.

Houston, Texas

They possess a feeling for material, a craftsman's pride in their skill to do it, and a profound musicianship: in the artist's sense; a feeling for music akin to that of the peasant weaver or embroiderer—a desire to create with the materials in which they work the most exquisite fabric possible. And that is precisely what they do.

St. Louis, Missouri

A typical day on tour started with a 9:00 a.m. departure from the hotel. We often had hundreds of miles to travel in one day on the bus. En route, we noticed that Rudi didn't stop immediately when we needed a rest break. He just kept driving, sometimes for a whole hour, much to our distress! Otherwise he was most helpful to a group of greenhorns from Austria. Rudi was not as well educated and polished as Mr. Tallerie, but by that time we knew a lot more about the United States of America.

Rudi was a good-natured man and an experienced driver. His driving skills were sorely tried on several occasions, however. On our way to Mt. Rushmore, Rudi was not sure he would be able to take the bus up the narrow, winding mountain road, but he was willing to try. Up and up he drove until we came to a tunnel. The bus was too high to fit through, so he could not continue. Papá told us to leave the bus, and Rudi backed down the narrow road to a place where he could turn around. After we reboarded the bus, he then drove us back to the little town where we found taxis to drive us back up the road right to the famous site. After all that effort, the sculptures of the four presidents were shrouded in thick fog. We could not see even the smallest detail of the giant portraits in stone. We stood in silence, disappointed that after all we did to get to this national monument, the presidents were hiding their faces. We said a short prayer.

Then to our amazement, the fog suddenly parted, and all the presidents were clearly visible. We could hardly believe our eyes. It was as if a curtain had been drawn back. The sun came out, highlighting the sculptures. It was like being in a show in an outdoor theater with a magnificent setting of rocks and pine forests. For a moment, we stood there, taking it all in. Then slowly the curtain closed, and the four presidents disappeared behind their shroud. All the effort to get there was worthwhile. In the meantime, Rudi had a little snooze in the bus at the foot of the mountain and vowed never again to try something of which he was not quite sure.

Another adventure was in Missouri where the roads are long and straight and the terrain is flat. There were few gas stations along the highway, so Rudi was driving as fast as possible. The roads were paved, but woe if anyone hit a soft shoulder. One day it happened to us! The bus suddenly went off the road and landed in the thick, sticky Missouri mud. Our bus was stuck deep in a muddy field beside the road. Rudi was frantic. He stepped on the gas, and the whole bus shook from right to left, like a ship on the high seas. We sat there with pale faces. No one said a word, but we wondered if Rudi would be able to pull the bus out of this mess. After a few anxious moments, which seemed like an eternity, the bus was back on the road, thanks to our excellent driver. Everyone sighed with relief.

Shortly after our first plunge into the Missouri mud, it happened again. This time, however, Rudi could not move the bus even one inch. It had sunk too deeply into the mud. A kind farmer came to our rescue with a team of sturdy farm horses. He had most likely rescued other cars before us. I thought, *Perhaps this is just part of life in Missouri.*

On the earlier tours, we had other challenges. We had to be extremely economical, so when we stopped at diners or cheap eating places, each of us could spend only twenty-five cents for lunch and thirty-five cents for dinner. If we had a long drive to the next concert town, we could not afford time for a lunch break and would have to eat at "Mitzi's Diner" on our bus. That was lunch bought, prepared, and served by our sister Maria, whose nickname was Mitzi. The family is eternally grateful to her for this sacrificial service!

Usually around 5:00 p.m., we arrived at the hotel. We checked in and went to our rooms. Everything was well organized, including the designation of each one's roommate. Then we ate at the hotel dining room or at a more economical cafeteria nearby. After dinner our driver took the concert luggage and two members of the family to the concert hall. There the instruments were unpacked: the spinet, the recorders, and Werner's viola da gamba. They needed to be at room temperature before being played. Two sets of concert costumes were unpacked and ironed. The rest of the family followed. We dressed, made up, and prepared to go on stage.

Backstage we could hear the murmur of the audience, which sounded like an ocean. The lights dimmed, the curtains parted, Father Wasner gave us the key, and—there was silence. One could hear that famous pin drop.

During the first portion of the concert, which included sacred music, madrigals and recorder selections, we wore long white dresses with black vests, while the men wore black suits. Then at intermission we changed to costumes of the type worn on Sundays and feast days in the Austrian countryside. This part of the concert always included songs and yodels from Austria and folk songs of many lands. We included favorites of the area in which we sang. So in America, we learned songs like "Home on the Range" and "My Old Kentucky Home." Often local managers brought us folk songs the night before a concert and asked us to perform them. In different countries these pieces were in foreign languages and had only one melody line. Father Wasner had to set the songs into more parts for us to sing, and we had to learn the language, text, and music by heart in one day's time. In this way, our program was greatly enriched.

An unexpected addition to our program occurred in one of our Christmas concerts in Town Hall, New York City. Johannes, almost four years old, was with us on stage as Mother introduced the family. When Mother said, "And this is Johannes," he turned to her and said, "Mother, I want to sing too." A bit embarrassed and certainly surprised, Mother said, "But, Johannes, do you know a song that you could sing?" "Oh, yes," he said loud and clear— "Old MacDonald Had a Farm." Mother replied, "Well, then, go ahead and sing." Town Hall reverberated with his "chick chick here and chick chick there." He knew every animal on the farm, and to the delight of the audience, he sang all the verses. At his last "oink, oink, oink," thunderous applause exploded from the audience.

Not understanding this sign of appreciation, Johannes was frightened and left the stage in a hurry. Backstage he announced to Rosmarie that if Mother asked him to sing again, he wouldn't do it.

Rosmarie did not take him seriously, so she failed to inform Mother of his strong feelings on the matter.

Our next concert was scheduled in Boston's Jordan Hall. Again, Mother introduced the family members one by one. She had been pleased that Johannes's solo was such a success in New York City, so after she introduced him, she added, "And now Johannes is going to sing for you." "No, Mother, I am not going to sing," he stated. "But, Johannes, I have told the audience that you will sing." Again he announced that he would not sing. Mother shrugged her shoulders and made a helpless gesture toward the audience. Then turning to Johannes, she said, "All right. Then you can go offstage." There was thunderous applause as the audience watched in rapt attention the struggle between Mother and her victorious young son.

After a typical concert, people from the audience would come backstage to compliment us on our performance. In some cities, there were receptions. As well meaning as these events were, we were sometimes so tired that we would have preferred to return to the hotel. Because we had to stand in a reception line and shake hands with so many people, we did not even get to eat. But it was touching to meet friendly and enthusiastic people throughout the country.

Papá was quite bored with shaking so many hands. Therefore, to amuse himself, he would count the people, in German, under his breath as they came through the line, making a gracious bow to each one. The audience members were thrilled when they met him because they thought he greeted them personally. Only Mother, to her amusement, actually heard Papá counting and understood what he was saying.

Then it was back to the hotel, and the next morning we left for the next city. Concerts were usually sung on consecutive days, except when the distances were so great that there was a day of travel between. Occasionally there was a day off when we could do laundry, mend stockings, shine shoes, and rehearse our music. Wherever we went we included sightseeing. Mother made sure of that, and in her conferences with Freddy Schang, she found out which important sights had to be seen on the next trip. We saw art museums, famous churches, extraordinary natural sites, and historic places. Had it not been for our extensive tours, we would never have seen these wonders.

On tour we children had our own fun occasionally. We composed a newspaper for our three authority figures: Papá, Mother, and Father Wasner. Johanna was the editor. We all got together in a hotel room to compose articles, poems, pictures, and cartoons of all kinds. In our newspaper, we tried to convey the thoughts and topics we felt

needed to be communicated to our elders but could not be said directly. They were hand-drawn on plain light-brown wrapping paper, larger than any magazine. Since we needed a free day to create these important pieces of literature, we did them only occasionally; no regular editions were possible.

Much laughter accompanied the creation of these newspapers, so much so that Mother once said she wished she could be part of the fun. "You'll have the fun when you read what we wrote," we told her. Mother had a good sense of humor, and she enjoyed our creations. One of the issues was in honor of Papá's sixtieth birthday in 1940.

We kept the newspapers for many years. To our dismay, they went up in smoke with many other keepsakes when our original home in Vermont burned in 1980. I still enjoy the memory of those rare days when we "children" got together for fun and laughter to create our family newspaper while on tour.

After our long tours, there were records to be made in New York City. Soon after we arrived in America, we recorded many of our songs for RCA Victor on 78-rpm records. Later we made records for the Concert Hall Society. We also recorded five albums for Decca Records. It was an exciting experience to work in recording studios of such high quality. Thank God for these records! By recording them, most of our repertoire—Christmas music, folk songs, recorder pieces, and sacred music—has been preserved and is readily available today. The recordings have moved along with modern technology and now appear as cassette tapes and compact discs for anyone who wants to know what kind of music the Trapp Family Singers really sang. Since the movie *The Sound of Music* gained such popularity, it could be easily assumed that the movie music was the type sung by the Trapps. Far from it!

During the early years of concertizing, we returned to our "borrowed" home in Merion, Pennsylvania, to spend our vacations. In the summer of 1940, the whole Trapp Family sat in the garden in Merion, having after-dinner coffee while we enjoyed the cool evening. As we looked up into the starlit sky, we saw a dome of light form above us with occasional flashes of green and red lights on the outer edges of the dome. The dome itself was white—as northern lights usually are. For about forty-five minutes we watched this awesome sight and followed every movement.

Northern lights are not common as far south as Philadelphia. Little did we know that very soon, we would be directed north to a permanent home for the Trapp Family in America.

Our New Home in Vermont

15

Our Green Mountain Home

After we had lived in Merion for approximately two years, Mr. Drinker had a chance to sell his little house. The Trapp Family had to find another summer home. The whole family had lengthy discussions about whether to rent a house or buy a piece of land. Renting seemed to us impractical and uneconomical. Every month we would spend our hard-earned money, and then it would be gone. If we bought a piece of land, we would spend the money once and then own the land, so we decided to buy.

When we lost our money in the bank failure in 1933, we were young. It then became a challenge for us to do things for ourselves that had previously been done for us. We quickly understood that there was great potential within each of us to meet this challenge, and we became a do-it-yourself family. In addition, a kind of pioneer spirit arose among us. I guess to my father's disappointment, we did not aspire to a South Sea voyage but instead talked about a farm where we would all work, build our own log houses, and plant vegetables and fruit trees. The idea of acquiring a farm was so firmly in our minds that when the ship that was to take us to America for the first time was named the *American Farmer*, we took it as a sign from heaven. Of course, the primary reason we had come to America had been to give concerts, but that did not dampen our dream of owning a farm.

Now that most of us were grown up, with ages ranging from two years to thirty years, strong and healthy, we considered buying a farm and operating it ourselves. It had been our dream, and it meant we could stay together. When we were still living in Aigen, Papá once talked to us about the subject of sticking together. As we were sitting in front of the fireplace, he took a stick and said, "Do you think I can break this stick in two?" We said, "Yes, Papá." He broke it in two pieces. Then he took several sticks in his hand and asked us again, "Do you think I can break these sticks apart?" We said, "We don't know, Papá." He tried it, and sure enough he could not break the bundle of sticks apart. Then he made the analogy: if we go in different directions, each one of us can get lost or get in trouble, but if we stay together, we will be strong. Even though this lesson may not have been in the forefront of our minds, we nevertheless felt we should buy a piece of land for the whole family to own together.

That summer of 1941, we rented a small tourist home called "Stowe Away" near the village of Stowe, Vermont, for the four months until the next concert season started. Since we had no home of our own to go to after that particular tour, we knew we had to find some land to buy before we went on tour. After spending the summer in Vermont, we knew we liked the Green Mountain area because it reminded us of Austria.

While Mother was in New York conferring with our manager, the family decided to pray for a place to buy. We set up a little altar in the Stowe Away, with a crucifix, two candles, and two vases of flowers, and took turns praying every hour for three days and three nights. After the third day, a man named Alfred Mausolf called on us to say that he had heard we were looking for property to buy. He knew of a farmer who had a farm in the vicinity of Stowe and might be willing to sell because it was too large for the farmer to handle alone. He had a family with seven little children, his wife was sickly, and no help was available. Mr. Mausolf offered to drive us to the farm so we could look at it. The farm, three miles above Stowe, was located on a hill overlooking three valleys. It had a view into a most beautiful landscape on three sides. The setting sun threw a golden hue over the fields and grassland. It was more than we could have dreamed or wished for! There was all the sun that Papá could ever want, and he loved the place.

When Mother came back from New York, we showed it to her. She agreed that it was the place for us, and we bought it in its entirety—with a loan—in 1942.

Our dream was fulfilled. The farm included a big maple orchard, meadows, a horse barn, a cow barn, a pigsty, and a chicken coop, all in poor condition. The premises were strewn with empty beer cans, bottles, and pieces of broken farm equipment. Yet we could look at the breathtaking view, and it quickly became our new home.

After we had been sitting in the bus, car, or train for a whole concert season, it was refreshing to move around in the clear Vermont mountain air and work on cleaning up the newly acquired land. We did not mind getting up at 6:00 a.m. and working until 10:00 p.m. We were building our new home! Rupert and Werner worked very hard to clean out all the junk from the old house, but they could not help us for long. On March 9, 1943, they had to leave for Camp Hale, Colorado, to serve in the Tenth Mountain Division as ski troopers. After some further training in Texas, both boys were sent into the area of Mount Belvedere in Italy to fight against the Germans. Rupert, who had been assigned to the medic division, later told me that he was so close to the Germans, he could actually overhear and understand their conversations.

When our brothers were inducted into the army, our family choir lost two important voices, Werner the tenor and Rupert the bass. But that did not stop us from giving concerts and continuing to tour. Father Wasner changed our program from mixed choir to a women's choir, although he occasionally sang a bass line with us.

Before the boys left, Werner promised that if they came home safely, he would build a small chapel on our property in thanksgiving. While the boys were in the army, we prayed fervently, asking God to protect them in their service to the country that had given us refuge. When Rupert and Werner returned to us in 1945, they received a joyful welcome during a session of our summer music camp. Rupert

soon left again to pursue his medical studies, but Werner built the little chapel on the hill behind our house, where it stands today. During the time that the boys were away, little Johannes and we girls worked together to build the new house after one section of the old one had collapsed in a blizzard.

Papá, Mother, and Johannes lived in another part of the old house that was still standing, but the rest of us slept in tents at the edge of the woods and in the hay loft in the horse barn. Camping is the name for this kind of accommodation. Camping was nothing new for us. We had done it years ago on an island along the shore of the Adriatic Sea. We knew how to go about it. It was a wonderful adventure.

People from the Vermont Nature Conservation Department told us they would give us saplings of pines, larches, and fruit trees if we were willing to plant them ourselves. We were willing, and they gave us about a thousand pine saplings and as many young fruit trees as we wanted. They even explained to us how easy it was to plant them: "Push a shovel upright into the ground to open up the soil, stick in the sapling, step on the ground where one opened it, and it is ready to grow on its own." We planted them, and they grew! Now, more than fifty years later, a forest of beautiful tall pines stands on the hill behind the Trapp Family Lodge. When I visit my family at the Lodge, I can hardly believe that we planted all of these trees.

In addition to trees, we planted a vegetable garden and a large strawberry patch. Papá and the boys learned to make maple syrup and worked the maple orchard in the early spring. The girls helped, and again, it was a wonderful time being in the woods. The result was three hundred gallons of grade A maple syrup the first year!

One necessity inevitably becomes vital, especially in the country—a cesspool. No matter what nice name one would like to give it, it is still a cesspool with the ditches that go with it. We learned that from Cliff, a villager who was evaluated as 4-F by the army and, fortunately for us, did not have anything much to do at home. Cliff knew the basics of living in the country and knew all about cesspools and their importance. He knew how wide, how long, and how deep it had to be, and most important in which direction the ditches had to flow. Once all that was established, we girls started digging.

For the first years we did not have or want electricity. Eventually, when guests appeared who were used to switching on the electric light when it got dark instead of lighting a kerosene lamp, the family felt we had better turn to the modern method of lighting our new home. That meant we needed permission from the county and the money to pay for it. The county officials told us if we dug the holes for the electrical poles, they would set up the poles and do the wiring. What a challenge! Because of the war, there was a shortage of men. Yes, we would dig the holes. We *girls* dug the holes, and the county gave us the electricity.

When the house was finally finished, it looked like an Austrian farmhouse similar to Gromi's Erlhof. Red and white geraniums in green flower boxes looked down from the balconies, and a little bell tower with a bell, on the roof above the entrance, completed our new home. The big living room had a cozy bay window where we could rehearse. There was enough space for our large family and the guests

1956

who started to arrive. No longer did we spend our vacations in borrowed places. We had a home, some of it built with our own hands.

Now we had a piece of land, a home, and the enthusiasm for it but not much time. We could work there only from June until the end of August. Then we had to prepare for another concert tour. When we came home from that concert tour, there was not enough money left after paying for our manager's fee and our publicity agent's fee and our hotels, meals, and transportation to see us through the summer months. What could we do?

Mother came up with an idea. Why not start a music camp? Once, when still in Austria, she, my sister Maria, and some other members of the family attended a music camp in the mountains. There they learned about the ancient recorders, how to play them, and where to buy them. Singing was also included in these camp programs. Why not do something like that in Vermont for music lovers during the summer months? A music camp would be beautiful for people on vacation, and it would give us a living through the off-season. The whole family liked the idea, and the Trapp Family Music Camp was on the map. Again, all fell into place.

Just at the time we considered starting the music camp, the abandoned Civilian Conservation Corps (CCC) camp in the valley below our property was about to be torn down. Papá and Mother applied for it, and it was leased to us for fifteen years. It had a fabulous setting, with barracks for the guests, a huge dining hall with an adjacent kitchen, an outdoor amphitheater, and several other buildings, which were needed to accommodate members of our family. There was also a barrack for a chapel, a gift shop, and a recreation hall. Perfect for our music camp! After our concert tour of 1943–44, we prepared the camp buildings for our guests. Advertising flyers went out and guests came in.

Father Wasner led the singing, and after three days, the voices of people who had never before seen each other melded into a beautiful choir. They could hardly believe it was possible to turn a group of strangers into a harmonious ensemble. But there it was. Some of the guests formed their own singing groups after they returned home. One such group was formed of guests from Boston, one from New York City, and one from Rochester, New York. These groups got together once a month in their respective cities to sing and reminisce about the wonderful time they had in the Green Mountains of Vermont at the Trapp Family Music Camp.

During each Sing Week (of ten days), two picnics were scheduled for our camp guests: one was on top of Mt. Mansfield, the highest mountain in Vermont, and the other on one of the large meadows on our property. The food for the picnics was provided not by a caterer, but by the camp kitchen headed by Johanna, and later by Lorli, and the kitchen crew. The crew consisted of ten seminarians from New York City, who were vacationing in Vermont. After the picnic, group singing and recorder lessons were conducted by my sister Maria.

Every evening after dinner, the guests assembled for folk dancing on the grassy area between the dining hall and the recreation hall. Everyone had fun while getting healthy exercise. The family provided music: Papá played the violin, Maria the accordion, and Werner the clarinet. Sometimes guests played additional instruments. Evening prayers in the chapel concluded the day. All the guests, staff, and

family joined in prayer and songs of thanksgiving.

These are only highlights of the program at the Trapp Family Music Camp. Many people came back year after year. Our camp became an institution for twelve years, ending then only because our tour schedule did not allow us to continue it.

Now the site of the camp is overgrown with trees, grass, and bushes. No one who had not been part of the music camp would ever know, when passing through, that once a music camp stood there, bustling with people, alive with music, fun, and laughter. There is no longer any physical reminder of the camp. Only the many guests who came to the summer music camp will remember the joys of singing and making music there.

In 1946, after our Christmas break, and just before we left for a concert tour that would take us clear across the continent to California, a letter arrived from Austria. It was from the chaplain of the American Occupation Army in Salzburg, and he told about the great need of the Austrian people after the war. Knowing that our family gave concerts in the United States, he asked if we would be able to do something to help our countrymen. Immediately we created the Trapp Family Austrian Relief, Inc.

During the next concert tour, Mother made an appeal to our audiences. We called it "Mother's Austrian Relief Speech." At the end of each concert, she would tell about the need in Austria. She would ask for donations of canned and dry foods, clothing, shoes, toys for children, and any usable items. She also asked for medicines such as aspirin and other commodities not available overseas, but readily bought here.

The response was overwhelming. Early in the morning after the concert, before our bus left, the donations arrived. Our audiences brought boxes and bags filled with food, clothing, toys, shoes, blankets, coats, and sweaters. In California a school sent a truck full of goods, which the pupils collected from their homes between two concerts. The effort and trust given to us were incredible.

At every stop on our concert tour, Mother made the same speech, and we received donations, which we stowed in the back of our bus. At the next opportunity, we obtained clean new flour bags, and while driving to our next destination, Werner stood in the middle of the bus transferring all items into these bags. At the next train station, we sent them by freight to Waterbury, Vermont. There, someone from our home staff picked them up and took them by pickup truck to the

Mother's Austrian Relief Speech

now empty music campsite. We stored the donations in the only barrack that was not in use when the camp was in session. The bags and boxes were piled up to the very ceiling and remained there until the next music camp started.

One particularly energetic camp guest, Mrs. Harper, realized the enormity of the work ahead even before these things could be shipped overseas. She took it upon herself to form a group of volunteers from the guests to sort and repack all these items. This wonderful group of people checked every item, then sorted and packed them into huge crates. These crates, donated by the Stowe Lumber Company, were made especially for this enterprise under the direction of our good friend Craig Burt. They were then sent to New York City where

Catholic Charities transported them along with other donations to Salzburg, to the attention of Chaplain Saunders, who with his staff distributed the contents to the needy victims of the war.

The cooperation we received once we started this relief work was miraculous. Donations continued to flow into the bus. Sometimes there was hardly any room for the family to sit. The bus was packed to the ceiling with precious cargo.

Then a letter came from Salzburg containing five thousand addresses. In the letter was a plea for American families to "adopt" one family or person in Austria and regularly provide life's necessities. Mother again announced the need after the concerts, and again, a miracle happened. We were overwhelmed, not only by the response of goods, but also by the generosity of the American people and their willingness to help a country other than their own.

There were official requests directed to us as well as private letters with pleas for special items that were not available in Austria anymore. Martina worked in the cellar for lack of another suitable place that was large enough to hold all the boxes of donations. There she labored to fill box after box with food, clothing, and other necessities, according to the directions given in these letters. These boxes had to be wrapped in a very specific way: in brown wrapping paper with strong string tied crosswise around them and with the address written on them in big letters. I learned to wrap packages in this perfect way prescribed by the United States Postal Service. This skill came in handy later after I left home.

When letters came to us, thanking us for clothing and supplies, we began to learn how badly war affects civilians. We had had no contact with friends or relatives in Austria during the war, and it was not until years later that we learned how our beloved Gromi had fared. When the Russians invaded Austria, Gromi, in her late eighties, was living with Tante Joan in the Martinschlössl, still owned by Uncle Bobby. On the way to Vienna and its surroundings, the Russians had to go through Klosterneuburg. Unfortunately they did their job well, entering homes, raping women, and stealing whatever they could.

Gromi had a loyal Hungarian servant named Loyosz, who

succeeded in keeping the household unharmed. Also with Gromi when the Russians arrived were Tante Joan and her friend Lisa, who was a nurse in Pakistan in her early years. She was the daughter of former Admiral Haus of the Austrian Navy. When the Russians entered the house and ordered everyone to the basement, Gromi went downstairs without a word, conducting herself with dignity. Tante Joan, trying to provide food for the duration, grabbed a loaf of bread and a knife as she went to the basement. When one of the soldiers saw the knife in her hand, he was ready to shoot her, but Lisa quickly intervened, saying in Pakistani, "The knife is only to cut the bread." The soldier, amazed to hear a language he understood, let Tante Joan go. He was from the same area in Pakistan where Lisa had been stationed. Coincidence?

The Russians left the area after a few weeks, but Gromi died shortly afterward. There was just enough time to bury her before the Russian troops returned. Gromi was buried with her daughter Agathe, our mother. Tante Joan and Lisa fled together on foot, pulling a *Leiterwagen* that held all their belongings. They walked almost the entire way, and it took them two years to reach Switzerland where Tante Joan owned a house.

We wondered at times how long we must keep up the Austrian Relief work, helping victims of the war in similar predicaments as Gromi and Tante Joan had been. Although we were glad to help, our Austrian Relief effort came to an end in 1950. We had concert tours in South America and Europe that same year, which included a stop in Salzburg. When we arrived in Salzburg, the station was filled with people. We did not understand why so many people were there. Then we saw familiar faces, and an official welcoming committee consisting of Archbishop Rohracher of Salzburg, Governor Joseph Klaus, and other dignitaries appeared through the crowd.

We met some of our school friends and Stutz von Jedina, our former playmate, who had become an attorney in Salzburg.[1] It was a great surprise for all of us to receive such an enormous welcome, but there was more to come. A few days later an official ceremony was arranged in the Aula, a large hall for official gatherings. The archbishop and the governor thanked us for our Austrian Relief effort. A poetess from the Salzburg area had written a special poem for our family, and she read it to us from the stage.

Little girls in dirndl dresses presented each of us with a lovely bouquet of alpine flowers. The next day, the festivities continued with Mass in the seminary where Father Wasner had been the music teacher, followed by lunch.

Werner's wife, Erika, had arranged three concerts for the Trapp Family Singers under the auspices of the governor and the archbishop. One concert was in the large concert hall in the Mozarteum. The second concert was staged in front of the cathedral, which was a special honor since our ensemble would be allowed to sing on the large stage where Jedermann (Everyman, a medieval morality play performed annually at the Salzburg Festival) was the only performance ever permitted. At that time, I was not aware of this special honor. As we stood on stage, my thought was, *Could they not have a found a smaller place to give us for this concert?* The third concert was held in the Kollegien Church in Salzburg.

Having been away from Salzburg for twelve years, we had the strangest feeling being back in the place that had been our home for fourteen years. The Nazi occupation had left its mark not only on the language but also on other aspects of life. We rented bicycles so we could go back and forth between our old home in Aigen, where we were staying, and the town of Salzburg. Unaware of the new traffic rules, we were stopped by a policeman when we tried to cross the main bridge on our bicycles. "Don't you know this is a one-way street? You cannot proceed," his firm voice said. I answered that we did not know since we had been away for twelve years. He looked puzzled and asked, "Where have you been?" "In America," I said. He was not sure whether or not to believe me. We wore the native Salzburg dress, and we still knew how to speak German. But after some discussion, he let us go.

We later experienced a similar incident. Chaplain Saunders, the man from the army who had corresponded with us, lent us a jeep to get around the area. Everyone there knew that jeeps belonged to the

American Occupation Army. An American officer stopped us because he suspected the vehicle was stolen. The officer interrogated us about why we were riding in an American jeep. Only after we mentioned Chaplain Saunders's name, and after we showed our American passports, did he let us go.

Times had changed so drastically, and yet everything still seemed so familiar. We had been given permission to stay in our old home in Aigen because the seminarians were away on vacation. Yes, it was the same house, but it was not the same. The order of priests who bought it after the war had renovated it to suit their needs; they had put in walls where there were not any before. Despite these changes in our former home, we appreciated the fact that we could stay there while we visited in Salzburg. Personally, I had no regrets that we did not live there anymore.

We retrieved some of our furniture that had been stored in different places in Salzburg by friends. Most of the pieces were so damaged that I suggested to Mother that they be auctioned and then we could use the money to buy clothing for the family. I was getting tired of sewing our dresses. She accepted this suggestion. We rescued only a few special pieces of furniture for ourselves and sold the rest. In addition, we gave many household items to our Austrian friends.

As long as we had lived in Salzburg, we had never eaten in a restaurant there. However, from showing our guests around town and visiting the castle, we knew that strawberries with *Schlag* (whipped cream) were served in the Castle Restaurant. Now that we were visitors in Salzburg, some of us decided that we would also enjoy this delicacy.

From Salzburg our concert schedule took us to Germany, Denmark, and Sweden. In Copenhagen, Erika, who had joined us in Salzburg, was asked to be the tenth member of our group because Rosmarie was sick at the time and our contract called for ten singers on stage. Erika consented with "trepidation" to sing in the second part of the program, which consisted of folk songs. Johannes remarked that Erika turned pale in spite of the makeup.

From Sweden, we went to Holland and Belgium before taking a

ship to England where we were booked in the Royal Albert Hall in London. England was the only country where Johannes was not allowed to play the recorder on stage because he was a minor.

In England it was apparent that our manager, Mr. Levitoff, had not done sufficient advance publicity; thus, some of our concerts were canceled. We had no money for our return tickets, so after a successful concert in Paris, Mother telephoned Mr. Schang in America. He purchased tickets for us on the *Liberté*. Since we had some free time until the day of our departure, Mother decided that the whole family should go to Rome. It was the Holy Year,[2] and she thought we might get an audience with Pope Pius XII.

We were granted the opportunity to sing for the pope during a general audience. It was held in a special room in the Vatican under the watchful eye of the Swiss Guard. The female members of our group wore long-sleeved black dirndls and black lace veils, and we performed Mozart's "Ave Verum" for the pope.

From Rome we went back to Paris, via Milan, for our departure on the *Liberté*. At the time, Erika, Werner's wife, had to return to her parents' home in Salzburg to pick up their baby and Rosmarie. The three of them were to meet us in Milan, to join us on the train going to Paris and on to Cherbourg. Their train was late arriving in Milan, and we had already left, but Werner had stayed behind to wait for Erika, Rosmarie, and the baby. They took the next train to Paris. In Lyon both trains were coupled together and, lo and behold, the complete family emerged in Paris from their respective coaches. Greatly relieved to be reunited, we spent the night in Paris, and the next day took the train to Cherbourg where we boarded the *Liberté*.

The crossing was uneventful until we hit the end of a hurricane. The ship rolled to such an extent that the portholes of the uppermost deck went underwater on one side, then shifted to the other side and continued rolling back and forth. The captain was said to have been concerned that the ship might remain lying on one side during one of these rolls. Everything was made as tight as possible in the dining room and salons. Many people disappeared into their cabins, and the crew ran around trying to help. One could not walk up or down the stairs without sliding helplessly into the corners. A priest was trying to say Mass in one of the salons, but suddenly in the midst of the service, the priest and the table, with all that was on it, fell over and slid along the floor. All activities were interrupted, and anyone who was still around was trying, somehow, to get where he or she wanted to go.

After a day of being tossed about by the severe storm, calm was restored, and we were able to continue on our voyage to the New York harbor. It was good to be home again in the United States of America.

16

A New Beginning

D uring our 1947 concert tour along the West Coast, we
noticed that Papá had become very quiet. He often retired
to the back of the bus to the bench, on which he stretched
out and went to sleep. Earlier he had seen a doctor of homeopathic
medicine in New York City, and the doctor told him to stop smoking,
which he did. His symptoms, though, did not improve. Papá was
always tired and seemed to lose his interest in life. Yet he came with
us on tour.

The trip back home seemed to take forever. One day Papá said he
felt especially tired. Since he also had developed a suspicious cough,
Mother suggested he fly to New York City to see the doctor who had
helped him before. He flew alone because we still had concerts on our
schedule.

Two weeks later Mother got a message from Papá, who was in a
hospital in New York City. She left immediately to go to his bedside.
When she arrived at the hospital, she was shocked at the terrible
change in him. He had lost fifteen pounds in two weeks, he was very
weak, and he wanted to go home. Privately the doctor told Mother
that there was nothing more he could do for Papá. He had lung
cancer, probably caused by the fumes in the early submarines. The
fumes were trapped in the engine room where the officers and crew
had to remain when doing underwater maneuvers, causing many of
the men to die of this treacherous cancer years later. The doctor said

that Mother should take Papá home to Stowe to spend his last days there. Papá was then sixty-seven years old.

When we arrived home following our last concert, the terrible changes in Papá's face were quite evident. We were glad we had brought home many potted, blooming geraniums to brighten his room. He lay in bed and could hardly talk. Mother had to feed him spoonful by spoonful. We visited with him only one at a time so we would not overstrain him.

My turn came; he asked me how my new bee colonies were coming along. That was the farthest thing from my mind, though he, in his agony, thought of my hobby. My tears flowed. I could not give him the answer; I was simply overwhelmed.

A few days later, on May 30, 1947, he died in peace, surrounded by all of us whom he had so faithfully protected our entire lives. He had always been there, like the air we breathe and the elements we never question. He went with us on tour in his quiet, gentle manner, ever mindful of our needs, as long as he lived. Papá now rests in our family cemetery, surrounded by lovely flower beds.

Only after all these years of struggle to make a new life in America have I been able to think in depth of my father's life with us. Yes, as great as he was during the First World War in the service of Austria's navy, he was even greater during the later part of his life, as the father of his singing family. He lived this new life with utter selflessness in this new and strange land.

Our concert tours continued without Papá, but we felt as if he were still with us. Each year we made two long tours throughout America, eventually singing in every state except Alaska. One season we gave concerts all across Canada. We sang in the Hawaiian Islands several times. In 1950 we traveled to South America for concerts where we sang in the Teatro Colón in Buenos Aires . That same year we returned to Austria.

We seemed to be away from home more than ever, but we had a small staff of faithful friends who remained in our house in Stowe. They attended to the guests who came to ski or to take their vacations among the Green Mountains. They kept the house in good order and forwarded our mail. Knowing that we were away from home for many months, the friends at home prepared a newsletter for our family. Our sister Rosmarie, who did not go on tour with us, and Mary Louise (Mary Lou) Kane, a young teacher who was working at the Lodge, were the writers and editors. These newsletters told all we possibly wanted to know: who came and went, the weather, and other bits of news. We read them in the bus while going from city to city, passing these reports around to everyone in the family.

Whenever we came home from our long trips, the home staff prepared a big welcome for us. It was wonderful to come back to a clean house, decorated for Christmas, and sleep in our own beds with clean sheets. How heartwarming it was to enjoy the meal prepared for the weary travelers and to return to such a grand home and friends!

But the breaking up of our family singing group was inevitable. Rupert pursued his medical degree, married, and raised a large family. He could no longer sing with us. In 1948, Werner had married Martina's friend Erika, but he still toured with us. Johanna married and left the group in 1948. That same year we took the oath of allegiance to become citizens of the United States of America. In 1951 Martina, who had married a year and a half before, died in childbirth. Then in 1954, Lorli married and began raising her family.

To continue performing as the Trapp Family Singers, we had to add non-family members to our group. The new members were gifted musicians who had voices similar to ours. They were all fun as travel companions, but of course, they had to be paid a salary, which reduced the family income. None of us family members ever received a paycheck for singing. The arrangement among us had been that we worked together, and each received what he or she needed. Mother had suggested this, and she called it "Christian communism."

The reviews were still favorable, and we were delighted by one in the *Philadelphia Inquirer* in December 1953 after our appearance with the Philadelphia Orchestra, directed by Eugene Ormandy. It read in part:

Undoubtedly this distinguished singing ensemble has no peers among any present day family vocal groups, if indeed there is any other such organization functioning in the field of music. . . . It is their authentic and indigenous singing, its unmistakable authority, its fine fullness, fervor and flavor which gives the Trapps their distinctive position. The vocal versatility of the Trapps, their wonderful coordination, unity, balance and blend of tone was magnificently displayed.

In 1955, the family made a long tour of New Zealand and Australia, stopping in Hawaii and the Fiji Islands to give concerts. The audiences were very receptive. In Honolulu, for example, a reviewer noted the "enthusiastic audience," and he praised "our impeccable singing" with "a subtlety of vocal blending which can best be compared to the most skillful orchestration." We were gone half a year, and everyone except Mother had the feeling that it was our last big trip. We had come to the end of our inner resources and endurance. Personally, I was sure of it. During one concert, I had a coughing spell that I could not suppress. I had to leave the stage, and I felt that it was the end of my singing in public.

For twenty years, we had sung with untrained voices. That was a feat in itself, simply surviving vocally through all those concerts. God had made this possible, and we served Him as well as we knew how. We realized—some sooner than others—that this mission of singing was over. It was time for a change.

When we returned to Stowe after the Australia–New Zealand tour, Mother asked us, "Do you want to go on tour once more? This time it would be to Japan." One by one we replied, "No, Mother, we do not want to go on another tour." Mother did not try to persuade us, but I know she would have loved to make that trip.

So, on January 26, 1956, in Concord, New Hampshire, we sang our very last concert. Through all the years of giving concerts, we performed in thirty countries. We "children" needed to further develop our personalities and potentials. We had been together for many years because of necessity and circumstances. We had functioned like clockwork with each doing his or her job, each

singing his or her part, with Mother winding the clock. It was time to step out on our own. As we went ahead into our new lives, we found out that God did not abandon us.

The Trapp Family Lodge had been Mother's dream come true. Ever since the director of the Vienna Choir Boys had told her that they operated a hotel in the Tyrol during their off-season, Mother had held on to this idea. At our concerts she invited the audiences, "Come to Vermont and enjoy a wonderful vacation at our farm." When I heard her say this, I thought to myself, *Where is she going to put all of these people?* The summer guests arrived regularly, beginning in the mid-1940s. Throughout those years, before we added additional guest rooms to the house, we children gave up our bedrooms to guests and moved to the third-floor attic to sleep. The nonpaying guests started depleting our small financial reservoir, even though they helped us with the work, so we started charging for board and lodging. Little by little, Mother engaged outsiders to help with the cooking, housekeeping, and serving of meals. There was a need for an office, which was placed just inside the front door. Our home had become a hotel. That was how the Trapp Family Lodge began.

When our concertizing came to an end, most of the family left the Lodge. Many of our paid workers were kind and loyal to Mother, but the mixture of the family doing the work and those paid to help and supervise did not fare well. Our home had become too large for the family alone and too small for the mixture of family, staff, and guests. Rupert, Johanna, and Lorli had left before the end of our touring. In 1956 I knew that it was time for me to leave the nest. I joined Mary Lou Kane in starting a kindergarten in Stowe. Two years later, after the town of Stowe introduced kindergarten classes into the public school, we moved our kindergarten to Glyndon, Maryland.

When we toured in Australia, the apostolic delegate of Sydney had asked Mother if some of the family would like to help in the missions. Mother was impressed with the idea and thought that she might start a school to train missionaries at the Lodge. After returning home from our Australian tour, we discovered that the money we had earned there could not be transferred to the United States, so the money was used to fund this mission trip. Mother, Father Wasner, Maria, Rosmarie, and Johannes left for New Guinea in 1956. Maria, Rosmarie, and Johannes were lay mission helpers in New Guinea, while Mother and Father Wasner traveled to various places in the South Seas on a fact-finding trip. The plan for the missionary training center never materialized. My sister Maria remained in New Guinea for thirty-two years, but Rosmarie and Johannes came back after two and a half years there. Johannes then studied history and biology at Dartmouth College and served time in the National Guard. Following that, he received a master of forest science degree from Yale.

Father Wasner stayed to work in the missions in Fiji for approximately five years. He was then sent to the Holy Land to be in charge of a papal mission. Later he was assigned to be rector of a seminary in Rome, Italy. Upon his retirement he returned to Salzburg, where he lived until his death in 1992.

After her return from the South Seas, Mother took several trips to

Austria, shopping for items for the Trapp Family Gift Shop. When she was back in the States, she spent much of her time giving lectures.

Even though Mother had the imagination to make the Lodge a beautiful place and had a soft spot in her heart for the guests, managing the hotel's finances was not her strongest point. She turned these duties over to Johannes, and he took over the running of the Lodge in 1969. Things went well for a time, but in 1980, tragedy struck.

On December 20, in the middle of the night, the Lodge burned to the ground. I was living and working in Maryland by then, and early on the morning of December 21, I received a call from Lorli. She said, "It happened last night. The Lodge burned down." The "it" she referred to was a dream that Papá had told us about. He dreamed that our house burned down, and we were all very busy, but he was not with us anymore. When Lorli said those words to me, I recalled the dream. Later, I heard details about the fire.

The Lodge was filled to capacity with guests, who were there for the holiday celebration and skiing. The temperature was below zero with a great deal of snow. Mother lived in a second-floor apartment, and her ninety-three-year-old secretary, Ethel Smalley, slept in an adjacent room. Mother, Ethel Smalley, and another friend were rescued by a heroic fireman who took them out on Mother's snowy balcony down an icy ladder.

When the night watchman discovered the fire, he ran through all the long corridors shouting, "Fire! Everybody leave immediately!" The guests responded and went out into the freezing temperatures in their nightclothes. At that very moment, the town of Stowe came to the rescue. People arrived from the other lodges with blankets and coats, offering to take in our helpless guests. Anyone who had an empty bed in his or her home showed up to give it to one of our shocked and freezing guests.

The fire department could not save the wooden building. A lack of water and the subzero temperatures made it impossible for them to do anything to save the Lodge. All the guests were accounted for except one man. He had gone back into his room to retrieve his wallet but did not make it back out. Johannes, who lived with his family down the road in a small farmhouse, came racing up in his truck. He could only stand there and watch the Lodge go up in flames.

Although I realized the devastating effect on so many people, I was not sorry to hear that our first home in the United States was destroyed. It had become too small and uncomfortable for guests to enjoy and for the staff to work in. For Mother, however, it was a terrible blow to see her life's work disappear. She never quite recovered from the shock.

In the morning, the rising sun looked upon a large heap of ashes, four chimneys, and the cement foundation that only the day before had held up the Lodge. Johannes, the president of the Lodge, then had to make a decision: to sell the property or to rebuild the Lodge. He chose to rebuild it and to make the new Lodge into the strongest and safest possible building. He would also make it a comfortable place where guests could spend their vacations. It would be a larger and more beautiful building, in the same style as the old Lodge.

With the help of an excellent local architect, Robert Burley, construction of the new Lodge began in 1981. On December 16, 1983, the new Lodge opened. When it became evident that many people were interested in taking extended vacations, Johannes agreed to add time-share chalets on the property down the road from the main Lodge. Mother lived long enough to see the completion of the new Trapp Family Lodge before she died in 1987 after a long illness, at the age of eighty-two. She was laid to rest in our family cemetery.

Strong in her beliefs, Mother lived her life passionately without compromise. Although she was not always easy to live with, I am grateful that she seized the opportunities that made it possible for us to share our musical talents with the world.

As I am writing this book, it occurs to me how things have changed for our family. After years of serving meals to our guests in the old Lodge, the family is now being served delicious meals at the new Lodge. We enjoy its beauty and hospitality.

17

Oh! The Sound of Music

W hat a variety of emotions *The Sound of Music* has created in all of us, upon whose life story the musical and the movie are based.

All over the world, *The Sound of Music* became one of the most popular movies ever produced. It made millions upon millions of dollars, and it made millions upon millions of people happy. Its story is forever imprinted into the hearts of those people who have watched this movie not once, not twice, but many times over. In Los Angeles a woman went to see it 58 times, a sailor in Puerto Rico 77 times, and a forty-seven-year-old woman from Wales was once listed in the *Guinness Book of World Records* for having seen it 940 times.

What makes the movie so popular when there are so many aspects that differ from our real life? I have given this question much thought. Perhaps the answer lies in the fact that it does not matter to people whether or not the story is true, but that it is a beautiful, wholesome story that appeals to the emotions of the viewers.

When I saw the musical for the first time, I cried. Others in my family were equally upset. The man on the stage in the naval uniform was not Papá. The play and later the movie, as beautiful as they were, misrepresented our life at home with our father. He was not some naval officer with a distant look and a boatswain's whistle in his mouth ready to order us children coldly about. In reality he was a dedicated father who saw to our well-being in every way. Among other things, he took us on picnics and camping trips, arranged schooling and music lessons, taught us some of the musical instruments, and made music with us. In fact while *The Sound of Music* shows our second mother teaching us the basics of music, thanks to our father we already had a repertoire by the time Gustl (Maria) arrived in our home.

The creators of the stage and movie versions made other changes, including altering the names, ages, and sequence of birth of us children. Because it involved the oldest Trapp daughter—in other words, me—I consider the scene with the song "Sixteen Going on Seventeen" to be a pure Hollywood creation. There was no important telegram delivered to our house by a teenage boy riding a bicycle.

The house in Salzburg used in the film was not our home; actually it was a former summer residence of the archbishop of Salzburg. Our villa could not be used because the religious order, to whom we had sold it, would not give permission. Also, we did not flee over the mountains into Switzerland. There is no mountain pass that leads from Salzburg into Switzerland. We simply took the train to Italy.

My father was a man of principle who wanted nothing to do with Hitler and therefore *did* refuse to fly the Nazi flag from our house. However, we were not directly confronted by the Nazis as dramatically as shown in the movie. Papá did not sing "Edelweiss" when we left. In fact "Edelweiss" is not the Austrian national anthem, as many people believe, but a song written for the play by Rodgers and Hammerstein.

All these things look impressive on the stage and screen, but they were not real. If our name had not been involved, I would have loved the movie, as all the other people did. But because our name was used and our life was portrayed inaccurately, I could not bear the thought of seeing the play and the movie more than once. I would not let them take away my memories.

As I said, I was not alone in feeling this way. Several of us children had the same reaction. My family is at heart a very private family, and only because of circumstances beyond our control did we stand on the stage and perform before audiences for twenty years. We are also sensitive to what is true and genuine and what is not. *The Sound of Music* did not pass our test.

We had no control over our portrayal in the musical partly because in 1956, Mother had sold all the rights to our story to a German movie producer. The unfortunate saga goes like this: one day someone offered Mother $10,000 for the rights to make a movie from her book, *The Story of the Trapp Family Singers.* An agent from the film company told her that if she would accept $9,000, they would give her the check immediately. Not realizing, at a time when she needed money, that she could have made a fortune with our story, she signed the contract and thereby sold all rights to the German film company for $9,000—with no royalties. That film company later sold the rights to the Broadway producers who wanted to make our story into a musical.

The Broadway musical *The Sound of Music* opened in New York on November 16, 1959, with Mary Martin as Maria and Theodore Bikel as the Captain. After the Broadway opening, the American producers felt it was wrong that we were restricted from getting any royalties. Mary Martin, Richard Halliday, and Leland Hayward were instrumental in seeing that Maria von Trapp received a very small percentage of the royalties. Mother gratefully accepted this unexpected windfall and shared it with Father Wasner and the nine remaining children. The Broadway musical won six Tony Awards, including Best Musical. The movie version, which was released in 1965, was awarded five Oscars including Best Picture and ranks among the most successful films in motion picture history.[1]

Millions of dollars did not flow into the pockets of the Trapp Family from *The Sound of Music*, but we have benefited greatly in other ways. As time went on, something happened that reconciled me with my "enemy," the play. The shift in my feelings actually came from those who saw *The Sound of Music*, loved it, and connected it with our name and family. Little by little, I met people on many occasions who recognized me by my last name and connected me with the musical. Their faces lit up, and I felt a wave of friendliness coming toward me.

I did not expect this result from the musical. Warmth and goodwill cannot be bought with millions of dollars. This is a matter of the heart.

Early in 1998, I received a phone call from a lady in New York City asking me to save the date of Thursday, March 12. The producers of *The Sound of Music* were reopening the musical on Broadway. There was to be an opening night gala performance at the Martin Beck Theatre, followed by a party. When the woman on the other end of the line mentioned the date of March 12, I blurted out, "That is the date of my eighty-fifth birthday!" As soon as the words slipped out, I wished that I had not said them, but she had already heard them.

I received an official invitation, and when the time came, my friend Mary Lou Kane and I went to New York City. I hardly recognized it after all these years since we had stepped off the boat to give our first concerts in America. The taxi driver wiggled and squeezed his vehicle through the heavy traffic. Right and left, cars and trucks inched past our taxi, but our driver managed to get through and deposited us at our hotel, the Doubletree Guest Suites, where the other invited guests were also staying. Upon arrival we were given delicious chocolate chip cookies—the biggest I have ever seen. The family arrived from Vermont and with them Hans van Wees, manager of the Trapp Family Lodge.

The gala performance was to be the next evening, March 12, so my family arranged a wonderful birthday lunch for that day at a Russian restaurant, the Firebird, near the hotel. It was a quaint and cozy little place with a doorman in formal Russian attire at the entrance. To my great surprise, Johannes gave me a birthday toast. I did not expect this honor, and I was deeply touched.

That evening we were taken to the Martin Beck Theatre in a limousine. When we arrived, the sidewalk was filled with people who were coming to the performance. The crowds were pushed to the sides to let us enter. The reporters squeezed through the crowd, and we saw flashes of light all around us from the cameras. To my surprise, I heard a reporter call my name. He turned out to be Chris

Olert, whose siblings Mary Lou had taught in our kindergarten. He was then working as a journalist in New York City.

We were seated near the front of the theater; the house lights dimmed, and the show began to the delight of the audience. During the intermission, I was asked to go up to the first balcony. It was difficult to get through the crowds, so Hans took me by the hand and plowed through the throngs and landed me at the right spot on the balcony. A surprise awaited me. I could not believe it, but there it was! A little boy in a sailor suit presented me with a huge birthday cake, iced with the words "Happy 85th Birthday." After the intermission, Hans escorted me safely back to my seat for the rest of the performance, which was a great success and received a standing ovation.

Following the show, a dinner was planned at the Tavern on the Green for the cast and invited guests. There was so much noise in the restaurant, with everyone celebrating the opening night, that I could hardly understand what anyone said, but it was all very wonderful.

Another special event connected to *The Sound of Music* took place on December 2, 1998. We von Trapps were invited to New York City to receive the Golden Decoration of Honor from the state of Salzburg for our Austrian Relief efforts following World War II. This lovely medallion is the highest honor bestowed by the state of Salzburg. The movie "children," who were also not children anymore, were presented the Mozart Medal for the part they played in *The Sound of Music*, which had brought an increase in the number of tourists coming to Salzburg. This December evening was the first time, since the movie came out in 1965, that we had come face-to-face with those who had portrayed us.

Two years later, another special occasion would bring me closer to my counterpart from the movie, Charmian Carr, who played the oldest von Trapp daughter. When her book, *Forever Liesl*, came out in the year 2000, Charmy came to Baltimore for a book signing, and we had dinner together. After introducing me to her audience, she read excerpts from her book, followed by a book signing. To my surprise, the people wanted my autograph too. Charmy and I sat side by side signing books. This evening was another moment when *The Sound of Music* touched me with its warmth.

After meeting so many people over the years who told me how they had derived such great enjoyment and inspiration from the musical and the movie, I finally came to terms with *The Sound of Music*. I thought, *Who am I, then, to criticize this movie?* After a long inner struggle, I finally learned to separate the memories of my life from the screenplay. I began to see that while all the details may not be correct, the creators of *The Sound of Music* were true to the spirit of our family's story. That freed me from my resentment and made it possible for me to enjoy the play, the movie, and the music as others have. I have even learned to sing and play "Edelweiss"!

18

Where Are the "Children" Now?

⚜♡⚜

*T*his question often comes from people who visit the Trapp Family Lodge. Oh, yes, the "children." It almost sounds like an afterthought. Where are they? What are they doing now that there are no more concerts to be sung?

It seems as though time has stood still. After twenty years of giving concerts throughout the Western world, we are still the "children." Why are we still thought of as children, although most of us were already grown up when we left Austria in 1938 to venture into the New World? Only the two youngest members of our family, Rosmarie and Lorli, were children at that time.

Year after year, from 1936 on, we gave concerts and traveled together from October until Christmas and went on tour again after Christmas until the end of May. This sameness of constantly being together as a family may have created even in us the feeling that we were still children.

As long as we gave concerts, we lived and worked together. When this phase of our lives ended in 1956, each of us had to find his or her own way of making a living. We had to part.

After Rupert returned home from the war in 1945, he realized that he needed to leave the singing group to follow his chosen profession.

He had completed his medical studies at the University of Innsbruck before we left Europe. He knew that if he wanted to practice medicine in the United States, he would have to receive a medical degree and do his internship in this country. He left home to attend the University of Vermont School of Medicine. He became a family doctor and married Henriette Lajoie, the daughter of a Franco-American attorney. They lived in Rhode Island and raised their six children there, all of whom are now married and have their own families. When Rupert retired, he moved back to Vermont, where he died in 1992 at the age of eighty; he is buried in our family cemetery.

Johanna discovered one day that she was already twenty-seven years old; her dream of becoming the mother of a large family of her own would slowly slip away if she remained in the singing group. In 1948 she married Ernst Florian Winter, whose father had been a city official in Vienna. Johanna became the loving mother of her large family of seven children. She died in Vienna in 1994, after all her children were married, and she is buried there with her oldest son.

Hedwig stayed at the Lodge for a short time after we stopped singing. She then left to teach first in Hawaii, then in a mountain community of Tyrol. When she came back from Austria, her asthma had become so severe that she was too sick to stay at the Lodge and not sick enough to go into a nursing home. She went to stay with Mamá's youngest sister, Tante Joan, who lived in a lovely little chalet on the lake of Zell am See, next to the Erlhof where Hedwig was born. Hedwig enjoyed a quiet, peaceful life with our aunt until she died of complications from her asthma in 1972.

Martina was seventeen years old when we left Austria. She wrote beautiful letters to her best friend Erika, who later became Werner's wife. Among the many guests who came to our music camp, Jean Dupire, a French Canadian, conquered Martina's heart. In 1949 they were married. When Martina was expecting her first child in April of 1951, she did not come with us on tour after the Christmas holiday but remained at home in Vermont. At that time, several concerts had been scheduled in California.

While in California, Mother received a telephone call from Stowe with the shocking news that Martina, then age thirty, and the baby had died during the delivery. We could hardly believe it when Mother told us. A silent heaviness settled upon us. We were so far away and could not even go home to lay our sister to rest. We had to give the scheduled concerts. Only Mother went home for this sad occasion.

Mother's first child, Rosmarie, felt uncomfortable on stage and left home to pursue other interests. She spent several years teaching in New Guinea. After some searching she eventually joined a religious group, the Community of the Crucified One, and joined a branch of the community in Vermont. There she settled down and started to enjoy life. Rosmarie helped to take care of Mother until her death in 1987 and also nursed a friend of Mother's until the friend died at the age of 101. Rosmarie now conducts sing-a-longs with the guests at the Trapp Family Lodge, which they enjoy immensely. The booklets that she made for these occasions include some of the songs from *The Sound of Music*, and these are popular choices of the guests who attend her sing-a-longs.

Eleonore, known by the family as Lorli, married Hugh Campbell in 1954 while we were still giving concerts. They had met at the music camp in 1947. Lorli and Hugh have seven daughters, who are all married with children of their own. Lorli is a wonderful cook and the happy grandmother of eighteen living grandchildren. She is also active with groups working to restore traditional family values in Vermont. The Campbell home, in Waitsfield, is a place where their closely knit family often gets together.

Johannes is president of the Trapp Family Corporation and presides over the Trapp Family Lodge. Johannes and his wife, Lynne, first met when she came to work at the Lodge in the summer of 1967. Lynne Peterson and a group of friends from St. Olaf College in Minnesota waited on tables and then sang and played in concerts for the guests of the Lodge in the evenings. Johannes and Lynne were married two years later in the stone chapel that Werner had built. They have a son and a daughter.

Werner married Erika Klambauer, Martina's classmate, whom he had already admired when we still lived in Aigen near Salzburg.

Martina invited Erika to visit us in our home in the Green Mountains of Vermont in 1948. Werner and Erika were married that same year, just before her visitor's visa expired. Werner traveled with us as our tenor until we sang our last concert in 1956, at which time he and Erika already had five children. Erika waited anxiously for him in Vermont while he toured. Werner and Erika left the family property and eventually bought a dairy farm in Waitsfield, Vermont. Erika, who had studied agriculture in Austria, was always Werner's faithful "right hand." There, on the farm, they raised their family of six children, and Werner worked the farm until his oldest son, Martin, could take it over.

In his retirement years, Werner has pursued various artistic endeavors. He began to weave beautiful carpets from the wool of his sheep, using his own designs, and crocheted many warm caps for a Native American mission school. He still improvises on his home organ at the age of eighty-six, while Erika tends her large vegetable and flower garden.

They are now grandparents of eighteen grandchildren. The four children of their youngest son, Stefan, and his wife, Annie, are showing signs of becoming a second set of Trapp Family Singers. The children, ages eight to fourteen, give concerts and have already made their first CD. I recently attended their first full-length concert in Foy Hall in Bethlehem, Pennsylvania. It was refreshing to hear how well they sang and harmonized. They were a big hit with the audience, receiving two standing ovations.

The oldest three children of Werner and Erika's second son, Bernhard, are also very musical. Bernhard's oldest son is planning to have a musical career and is studying the cello in college.

Werner and Erika's second daughter, Elisabeth, embraced music as her profession. Elisabeth has come to be identified as much as an art song singer as a folksinger and has also begun to make a mark with her original compositions. She has given concerts as a soloist across the United States as well as in Canada, Austria, and Russia.

My twenty-eight nieces and nephews all have interesting lives, but space limitations prevent me from delving into the stories of their families. Therefore, I have mentioned only those who have a musical connection.

My sister Maria, the second daughter of Georg von Trapp, went to New Guinea as a lay missionary after we stopped giving concerts. She has many wonderful and interesting stories to tell. She worked with local youngsters and also taught English in a mission school. She formed a choir with the schoolchildren who sang beautifully for their church services and other occasions. Maria remained there for thirty-two years with two brief interruptions for vacations in Vermont.

Now Maria is living in a little house in the woods on the Trapp Family Lodge property. Occasionally she acts as hostess for the guests who want to meet one of the "real" members of the Trapp Family. She loves to play the accordion, which Papá taught her, and she plays for the delight of guests, friends, and family. Her repertoire consists of marches, dances, and songs, some of which she composed. Everyone who meets her loves her. Maria is now in her late eighties.

You must be wondering what I did after our singing group disbanded. In 1956 I left the Lodge with a friend, Mary Lou Kane, who had worked with us there. Together we started a kindergarten, first in the town of Stowe and later in Maryland. We retired in 1993 after conducting our kindergarten for thirty-seven years. We now share a lovely apartment in the suburbs of Baltimore, Maryland. As retired people seem to be, we are always busy. We enjoy our retirement because we can do things we did not have time to do before.

Over the years, I turned some of my sketches into watercolors, enough in number to have several exhibits, including one in the Austrian Embassy in Washington, D.C. Many of my paintings were sold, but I kept some that now adorn the walls of our apartment.

Among other interests, I now spend time writing, making music, singing, playing the piano and guitar, and visiting family members. Looking back, at the age of eighty-nine, I am thankful that my life has been so rich with many unusual and interesting experiences. I wouldn't have wanted it any other way.

Each one of the "children" would have enough stories to fill his or her own book. In this book, I can only briefly outline each one's life. We still keep in touch with one another and get together at the Trapp Family Lodge for weddings, anniversaries, and other special occasions, with Johannes always our gracious host. He makes sure that family members who do not live in the vicinity of Stowe have accommodations at the Lodge for these festivities. Occasionally we get together for an afternoon in Werner and Erika's home, for a dinner in Johannes and Lynne's house, or in Maria's cozy little house in the woods to reminisce and share family news. Invariably someone starts a song, and others join in, one song following another.

We still sing and sound almost as good as in years past, even though we're not a full choir anymore. Singing has not departed from our lives, and the sound of our music will never fade away as long as some of us can get together. Yes, we still love to sing.

Notes

Chapter One: The Captain, Our Father

1. *Ritter* means "knight" and *von*, which is placed before one's last name, is an aristocratic title that is bestowed upon a person who has done an extraordinary service for his country or fellowman. Only the emperor can give this title, which is accompanied by an elaborate document.

2. Pola was the most important harbor in the Austrian monarchy and would become part of Italy after World War I. The city is now part of Croatia, and the spelling has changed to Pula.

3. Fiume was an industrial city on the Adriatic Sea; it is now Rijeka, Croatia.

4. This was the beginning of what would later be known as the Boxer Rebellion (1900–1901). The Chinese people involved were called Boxers because they practiced martial arts.

5. The Chinese government officially supported the rebellion.

6. Edwyn Gray, *The Devil's Device: The Story of Robert Whitehead* (London: Seeley, Service & Co., Ltd., 1975).

7. Today this home still exists, but our family no longer owns it.

8. This book, written in German, is currently out of print: *Bis zum Letzten Flaggenschuss* (Until the Last Salute).

Chapter Two: Mamá, Our Sunshine

1. The English equivalent of her name is Agatha, and that is how people in English-speaking countries pronounce it.

2. A seaside town near Trieste, which at that time belonged to Austria.

3. The Bosnian soldiers were sent to help at my widowed grandmother's farm by the Austrian government. This was in gratitude of my grandfather's contribution to the war effort.

Chapter Three: Life with Gromi

1. This castle remains in existence today and is now a cultural center in lower Austria, owned by Gromi's great-nephew.

Chapter Five: The Postwar Era

1. The word *Dragoner* comes from a certain Hungarian regiment that was known to be ruthless and was called "Die Dragoner." This name seemed to fit her personality!

Chapter Six: Years of Change

1. Mamá died during the late evening of September 2, 1922.

Chapter Seven: Our New Home Near Salzburg

1. The park and the Ferris wheel remain in existence today. Even the Nazis left everything intact.

Chapter Ten: Adventures with Papá

1. Boats with a wooden frame covered with rubberized canvas; all could be dismantled, folded, and stored in a bag.

Chapter Twelve: The Invasion

1. An aunt of Maria's classmate who lived near St. Georgen.
2. A shrine in the vicinity of Salzburg.
3. Private taxis in Aigen.
4. A priest at the Boromaeum.

Chapter Fifteen: Our Green Mountain Home

1. Dr. Hermann Ritter von Jedina became an attorney for the government of the State of Salzburg.
2. Every twenty-five years, the Vatican declares a Holy Year to emphasize the Christian way of life. Many people make pilgrimages to pray in Rome at that time.

Chapter Seventeen: Oh! *The Sound of Music*

1. Artistic license won out over historical accuracy as both the play and the movie *The Sound of Music* were developed. Both are interesting stories, basically true to the spirit of the family, but the fact remains that the story lines depart from the actual events. Briefly stated, here is the evolution of the play and the movie:

Maria von Trapp published *The Story of the Trapp Family Singers* in 1949. Hollywood showed interest—but only in the title! And Maria wasn't interested in an offer only for the title; clearly the whole story was important to her. The German film company to whom Maria sold the rights in 1956, for the paltry sum of nine thousand dollars, made *Die Trapp Familie* and eventually *Die Trapp Familie in Amerika*, which were successful in Germany and later in other European countries and South America.

An American director, Vincent Donahue, saw the first German film and pursued the idea of turning it into a musical for Mary Martin, who then, with her husband, Richard Halliday, and producer Leland Hayward worked out a rights deal with the German producers. They chose Russel Crouse and Howard Lindsay to write the play. They wanted to use primarily music sung by the Trapp Family with one new song written by Richard Rodgers and Oscar Hammerstein. But Rodgers and Hammerstein envisioned a completely new score, and Hayward and Martin agreed. It was, in fact, the final collaboration of Rodgers and Hammerstein, opening on Broadway in 1959, and became the second-longest-running Broadway musical of the 1950s.

The 1965 movie was a Robert Wise production for Twentieth Century Fox; Fox bought the movie rights to *The Sound of Music* from the German film company (according to www.germanway.com/cinema/som_main.html). Ernest Lehman wrote the screenplay. Maria von Trapp met with Lehman to discuss the script because she was not pleased with her husband's portrayal in the play and hoped that the movie would be more realistic and true to him. The script remained as Lehman wanted to write it, however. The movie featured Julie Andrews as Maria and Christopher Plummer as the Captain.

About the Author

Agathe von Trapp was born in Austria in 1913, the oldest daughter of Baron Georg von Trapp and his first wife, Agathe. She is one of the original Trapp Family Singers, a world-famous choral group that performed in thirty countries. Their story was the inspiration for *The Sound of Music*. With her family, she recorded with RCA Victor and Decca Records, as well as participated in the operation of the Trapp Family Lodge and the summer music camp in Stowe, Vermont.

A gifted artist, she has had her work exhibited in Europe and America. Her work illustrates *The Trapp Family Book of Christmas Carols* (Pantheon) and appears in other books and publications.

Following her twenty-year singing career, Agathe von Trapp assisted in the operation of a kindergarten near Baltimore, Maryland, for thirty-five years, and two years in Stowe, Vermont. Now retired, she continues her interest in art, history, and writing. In her memoirs, *Agathe von Trapp: Memories Before and After The Sound of Music*, Agathe shares the true story behind the film legend.